Genesis

The Beginning, The Fall
And The Promise

Written and illustrated by Jeff Todd

Genesis:
The Beginning, The Fall And The Promise

Published by:
Jeff Todd
Newnan, Georgia

ISBN-13: 979-8-3304-9422-4

The purpose of this book is to share the Good News of Jesus Christ and put it out there in an easy-to-understand way. It is part of the outreach ministry of Jeff Todd.

Please note that there will be mistakes and misprints in this book. We are all human, right? We hope you won't find too many of them. This book was edited to the best of the author's ability and he will not be held responsible for errors.

Direct all correspondence to:

A BackPew Review
c/o Jeff Todd
PO Box 71972
Newnan, GA 30271-1972

Contents

Introduction

As we probably already know, Genesis is the first book of the Bible. It's in the Old Testament section in the front - right after the book cover. It's fairly easy to find.

Genesis was written around 1450 – 1410 B.C. by a man we all have heard of before... Moses. Ring a bell? I thought so. It is a well-known book because it provides us with the story of creation. It tells us how, life as we know it, all began. It gives us God's original 'perfect' plan for humanity and life, while revealing the freedom He gave us to make our own choices on how we want to live it. We learn the person and nature of God (as Creator, Sustainer, Judge and Redeemer) and the value of human beings (made in God's image, saved by grace and used by God in the world). We also learn what happens when we sin (the fall, the separation from God and His judgment). Importantly, we learn about hope (God's promises, forgiveness and the promised Messiah).

From the story of Adam and Eve, we see how sin can manifest its way into our lives and how it begins weaving its destructive webs into the lives of others. Generations become affected by sin. From Genesis, we see how God dealt with this problem with a flood. By destroying everyone on Earth, except a small family led by a man named Noah, life began again.

For most of us, we are familiar with the stories of Adam and Eve and Noah. But, what we may not know, is that there are other stories in Genesis. Have you heard about Abraham, Isaac, Jacob and Joseph? These are generations of men that God made a promise to. Their story is how God used them to create a large nation. The funny thing is that God created numerous descendants from a man that was really too old have children anyway. It was an impossibility made possible by God.

Genesis is an important book because it contains a lot of history. There are genealogies listed within the chapters that may cause readers to become bored by reading them. But, they are equally important because it gives the history of Israel. Many tend to skip this part, but know that our family branches originated from this family tree somewhere down the line. That makes their story part of ours, too. That makes it personal.

Many people consider Old Testament books a little boring. They're too long to read. The characters' names are hard to pronounce and remember. And to some, none of it makes sense. I'll admit, some of Genesis was a little hard to understand. Many times I had to read a verse more than once (or read it slower) to get a better understanding of it. This guide, that you hold in your hand, is what I received from reading the Book of Genesis. I had some struggles, but I worked them out. I hope it helps you.

Today we are going to begin reading the Book of Genesis from start to finish. If you're reading A BackPew Review for the first time, the large bold title at the top middle of some pages are the chapters. The smaller bold titles are what I like to call 'sub chapters'. And the scripture under them is for reference. This will let you know where we are reading from so that we can follow along together. You should find this in your Bible and read it first before reading from this guide.

This should be fun. If you get tired, put it down and start again tomorrow. Let's enjoy the Bible together. That's the way it was intended. Are you ready? Grab your Bible because you will need it. Let's begin...

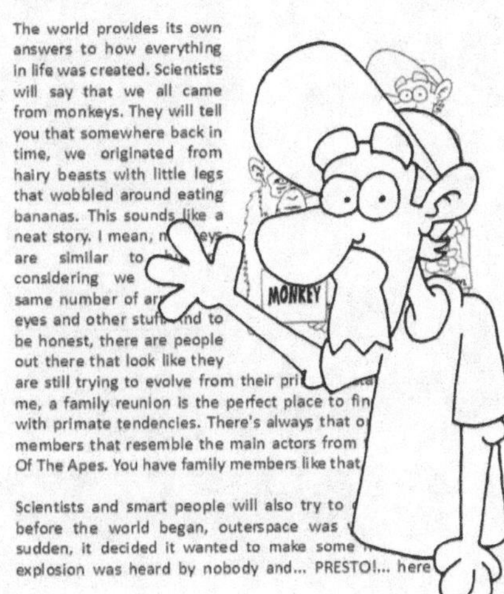

The Story Of Creation

The Beginning
Genesis 1:1 – 2:3

The world provides its own answers to how everything in life was created. Scientists will say that we all came from monkeys. They will tell you that somewhere back in time, we originated from hairy beasts with little legs that wobbled around eating bananas. This sounds like a neat story. I mean, monkeys are similar to considering we same number of ar eyes and other stuff and to be honest, there are people out there that look like they are still trying to evolve from their pri me, a family reunion is the perfect place to fin with primate tendencies. There's always that o members that resemble the main actors from Of The Apes. You have family members like that

Scientists and smart people will also try to before the world began, outerspace was sudden, it decided it wanted to make some explosion was heard by nobody and... PRESTO!... here

9

The Story Of Creation

The Beginning
Genesis 1:1 – 2:3

The world provides its own answers to how everything in life was created. Scientists will say that we all came from monkeys. They will tell you that somewhere back in time, we originated from hairy beasts with little legs that wobbled around eating bananas. This sounds like a neat story. I mean, monkeys are similar to humans considering we have the same number of arms, legs, eyes and other stuff. And to be honest, there are people out there that look like they

are still trying to evolve from their primitive state. If you're like me, a family reunion is the perfect place to find these humans with primate tendencies. There's always that one or two family members that resemble the main actors from the movie Planet Of The Apes. You have family members like that, too?

Scientists and smart people will also try to convince you, that before the world began, outerspace was void, and all of a sudden, it decided it wanted to make some noise. BANG! An explosion was heard by nobody and... PRESTO!... here we are today. Somehow this major explosion created the universe and everything that currently lives in it. I don't know. Most explosions that I have seen or heard were usually destructive. It usually tore stuff up and left little chunks lying around all over the place. No new life was created... that's for sure.

And then there are those deep-thinking brainy people that say we all came from aliens. In a far away planet somewhere, intelligent life decided they wanted make something cool to look at. I guess the thought floated around and someone in the group came up with the brilliant idea of creating a place called Earth, and to add some moving creatures, they formed humans and animals out of some kind of intergalactic space dust. The story sounds cool to me. But, even with a story like that, you have to wonder, "Who created the aliens?" Right?

There are many other thoughts and beliefs out there of where it all began. I personally like the version from the Bible. I believe God created everything. It just makes more sense. From the first chapter and first verse of Genesis, it gives the basics. From day 1 to Day 6, everything is basic. It doesn't get into the details of how He did it, but it simply tells us that He did and how long it took Him. That's enough for me. But, if you insist on seeing the details of His creation, and you should, you will see complexity in everything. Try counting the stars and see how big the universe truly is, look at the large variety of living creatures (every one is unique) or put anything God created under a microscope and you will see the finer details that will blow your mind. God is creative and places a lot of detail in His creation. This would mean that He places great value in it. Look at the human body and look deeper into how everything works effortlessly. That should be enough evidence to know God exists and that He loves us.

Day 1 was the beginning of something awesome. God created the heavens and the earth. It had no form to it and it was pretty much empty and dark. It did mention that there were plenty of water, but I'm sure the human eye couldn't see it. It was dark. On the same day, God created light because He said, "Let there be light!" This is where we get our 'day' and 'night' from. We also get our 'morning' and 'evening'. It all happened right here on the first day of creation.

Either God got bored seeing all of that water or He was preparing something special for His greatest creation that was yet to come, because on Day 2, He created the sky. It was placed up high while the water was placed down low, yet both of them work together to sustain life as we know it. This is my simple-minded synopsis: The sun heats the water causing it to evaporate into the sky. This process creates clouds. Clouds produce rain. Rain falls to the ground. And this process repeats itself over and over and has been working great for thousands of years. Pretty cool, huh?

Day 3 was exciting. God caused land to appear from the water. We're talking about dry land – not mud. This is where we get our continents with its countries, states and cities. This is where we also get our exotic islands that many of us dream of taking a cruise to one day. Unfortunately, back then, these weren't tourist attractions yet. Tourists weren't invented on Day 3, but they were on the way. Also, on Day 3, God created vegetation. You know, stuff like leafy foods – like turnip greens, collards, lettuce and cabbage - and fruits that grow from a tree. Each plant and fruit had seeds built within so that it could reproduce itself. It kinda makes you wonder why we have certain fruits today that don't have seeds – such as grapes, watermelon and oranges. I have a funny feeling that man had something to do with this. I'm not a farmer or an agricultural scientist, but maybe these have been modified with man-made chemicals that dissolves seeds. I guess people got tired of spitting out seeds and said, "Hey! We got to do something about this. Squirt

some of that icky stuff on this and see what happens." It might be worth looking into.

God created the sun and moon on Day 4. The purpose was to separate the day from the night. It also served as a way for us to determine the seasons – Fall, Summer, Spring and Winter. To elaborate on this a little, we know if July is coming in a couple months, we know to go ahead and stock up on shorts and flip-flops because we expect it to be hot outside. The same applies for January because, based on years of experience, this is a cold month. We better get our coats and thermal underwear out of storage because, chances are, we will be freezing our butts off if we don't.

As an added bonus, because of the creation of the sun and moon, people could tell what day and year it was by counting how many times the sun rose. I'm sure, years down the road, someone caught on to this neat thing God created for us for free and decided to exploit it by inventing calendars and watches for monetary gain. Yes, it makes it easier to keep up with special occasions by looking at a calendar because counting sunrises can be difficult and it might be hard to keep up with. Imagine keeping up with your wedding anniversary with your spouse with the use of the sun.

"Honey, surprise! Today is our anniversary. Where's my gift?"

"No... I don't think so. I only counted 172 sunrises this year. You're a few days off, dear."

"No. I'm SURE today is our anniversary. You must have miscounted the sunrises again. You always forget our anniversary. You don't love me."

"I didn't forget. Of course I love you. I was only joking. I bought your gift days ago. All I got to do is go pick it up. I'll be back in a couple of hours."

<Wally World trip>

Day 5 was a very busy day. God created the creatures of the sea — like fish, dolphins, whales and things with fins. He also created the creatures of the sky — birds, bats, eagles, owls and other things with wings. The cool thing is that He told them all to be fruitful and multiply. That means 'make babies' and populate the Earth. If you look at the numerous types of sea creatures and birds that fly in the air, you will see that there are all kinds of types.

God could've created 'a bird' and said, "That's it. Just one bird — we will call it a 'bird'. It has a beak. It has wings and little birdy legs. We'll give it feathers, but nothing special. Just one type of bird — maybe with brown feathers and a white belly. That's it. I'm done with birds. Let's move on to something else." But, He didn't.

There are all kinds of birds with special unique features that make it special. Have you ever noticed how beautiful a parrot is with it's colorful feathers? It's a remarkable work of art. God made these and He made them for us. I think that's pretty cool. And what about the fish? Visit a local aquarium one day and see the different varieties. It will blow your mind. God is awesome like that.

God focused on the land on Day 6. He created livestock, animals that moved along the ground and wild animals. Here again, there are different kinds and color types. Each animal is unique. That's for sure. Try comparing a dog and a cow. They are totally different. What about a jaguar and a sloth? Not only do they look different, but they work on different speed levels. Jaguars are fast animals and sloths are just way too slow, but they are cute to look at.
Maybe that's the point. God gave us variety.

Also on Day 6, God created man – man and woman. But, with man, He made them a little special. The Bible says He created them in His own image. He also gave them the power to rule over all of the other animals. He told man to eat from all of the seed-bearing plants and trees that bore fruit with seeds. The great thing about knowing this is that God wanted to make sure that man had everything he needed before He created them. It's like He planned everything for His greatest creation – and that is us. That's love right there.

What does it mean to be 'made in the image of God'? The Bible says we are made in His image, right? If you look at the people living in the world today, you will notice that everyone looks unique – different from one another. It's probably a good thing because I'm sure we wouldn't want to look like some people we know. But, to be 'made in the image of God', it would have to be something other than our outward appearance. Here's what I discovered:

The 'image of God' refers to the immaterial part of humanity. It sets human beings apart from the animal world, fits them for the dominion God intended them to have over the earth (Genesis 1:28), and enables them to commune with their Maker. It is a likeness mentally, morally, and socially.

Mentally, human beings can reason and choose. This is a reflection of God's intellect and freedom. Anytime someone invents a machine, writes a book, paints a landscape, enjoys a symphony, calculates a sum, or names a pet, he or she is proclaiming the fact that we are made in God's image.

Morally, humanity was created in righteousness and perfect innocence, a reflection of God's holiness. God saw all He had made (humanity included) and called it 'very good' (Genesis

1:31). Our conscience or 'moral compass' is a vestige of that original state. Whenever someone writes a law, recoils from evil, praises good behavior, or feels guilty, he or she is confirming the fact that we are made in God's own image.

Socially, humanity was created for fellowship. This reflects God's triune (three in one) nature and His love. In Eden, humanity's primary relationship was with God (Genesis 3:8 implies fellowship with God), and God made the first woman because 'it is not good for the man to be alone' (Genesis 2:18). Every time someone marries, makes a friend, hugs a child, or attends church, he or she is demonstrating the fact that we are made in the likeness of God.

Part of being made in God's image is that Adam had the capacity to make free choices. Although they were given a righteous nature, Adam and Eve made an evil choice to rebel against their Creator. In so doing, they marred the image of God within themselves, and passed that damaged likeness on to all of their descendants (Romans 5:12). Today, we still bear the image of God (James 3:9), but we also bear the scars of sin. Mentally, morally, socially, and physically, we show the effects of sin.

I thought that was a good definition of being 'made in the image of God'. How about you?

The Bible says that God 'rested' on Day 7 and made this day 'holy'. After He created everything in six days, He said, "Everything was good." He was happy with what He created and decided that He would rest. Was He tired? I seriously doubt it. Everything He created was done verbally (by word) and not physically. Here's what I found:

In Genesis 2:2 we read, "And on the seventh day God ended his work which he had made; and he rested on the seventh day from all his work which he had made." If God is omnipotent—if He has all power—it doesn't make much sense that He would need to 'rest'. After we've had a busy week, we take a nap—but God?

First, we should quote the verse correctly. It doesn't say God 'needed' to rest; it simply says that He did rest. Also, it is clear from Scripture that God did not rest because He was tired. Genesis 17:1 calls God the 'Almighty God'. Psalm 147:5 says, "Great is our Lord, and of great power: his understanding is infinite." God is all-powerful; He never tires and never needs to rest. As Isaiah 40:28 says, "Hast thou not known? hast thou not heard, that the everlasting God, the LORD, the Creator of the ends of the earth, fainteth not, neither is weary? there is no searching of his understanding." God is the sum of perfection; He is never diminished in any way, and that includes being diminished in power.

When God said, "Let there be light," the light appeared. He simply spoke creation into existence (Genesis 1:1-3). Later, we read that Jesus Christ "Who being the brightness of his glory, and the express image of his person, and upholding all things by the word of his power, when he had by himself purged our sins, sat down on the right hand of the Majesty on high." (Hebrews 1:3). Forget the image of Atlas straining under the weight of the world on his shoulders. It's not like that. The entire universe is held together by Jesus' word. The creation and maintenance of the universe is not difficult for God. A mere word will suffice. As Psalm 33:9 declares, "For he spake, and it was done; he commanded, and it stood fast."

The Hebrew word translated 'rested' in Genesis 2:2 includes other ideas than that of being tired. In fact, one of the main definitions of the Hebrew word shabat is 'to cease or stop'. In Genesis 2:2 the understanding is that God 'stopped' His work; He 'ceased' creating on the seventh day. All that He had created was good, and His work was finished.

The context of Genesis 1–2 strongly affirms the idea of God's 'rest' being an ending of work, not a reinvigoration after work. The narrative tells us which things God created in each of the first six days. His power is displayed through the creation of light, mountains, seas, the sun, moon and stars, plant and animal life, and, finally, humanity. There are many parallels between the first three days of creation and the second three days. However, the seventh day is a sharp contrast. Instead of more creating, there is shabat. Instead of God 'doing' more, He 'ceased' from doing.

God did not merely 'rest' on the seventh day; He 'stopped creating'. It was a purposeful stop. Everything He desired to create had been made. He looked at His creation, declared it 'very good' (Genesis 1:31), and ceased from His activity. In the Jewish tradition, the concept of shabat has been carried over as the 'Sabbath'. The Law of Moses taught there was to be no work at all on the seventh day (Saturday). Because God ceased from work that day, the Israelites were to cease from their work on the Sabbath. Thus, the days of creation are the basis of our universal observance of a seven-day week.

Simply put, God's 'rest' was not due to His being tired but to His being completely finished with His creative work.

Pretty interesting, huh?

The Story Of Adam

Adam and Eve
Genesis 2:4 – 2:25

As we have already read, God created man on the sixth day. This was after He had created everything else. The Bible tells us that He formed him from the dust of the Earth and breathed into his nostrils the breath of life. At this point, man became a living, breathing being. He was a brand-spanking new creation – full of life - healthy and stress-free. This tells us that there's nothing fancy about the chemical composition of the human body. It is when God breathes the 'breath of life' into it that it brings forth life. And when He decides to remove it, the body dies and goes back to the dust it originally came from. Ashes to ashes, dust to dust.

God placed him in a garden area that He created, which was in the east in a place called Eden. This place was special. It had all kind of trees that were pleasing to the eye and good for food. I imagine a beautiful orchard with all kinds of fruit trees –

apples, pears, oranges, peaches, plums and probably every kind of fruit tree imaginable was there. Can you visualize how beautiful this would be? It would be like a rainbow of food within reach. It sounds nice, doesn't it?

The Bible tells us that in the middle of the garden were two trees with specific names. One was the 'tree of life' and the other was the 'tree of the knowledge of good and evil'. It doesn't tell us if either of these trees had fruit on them yet. All we know is that they are just trees. Keep reading.

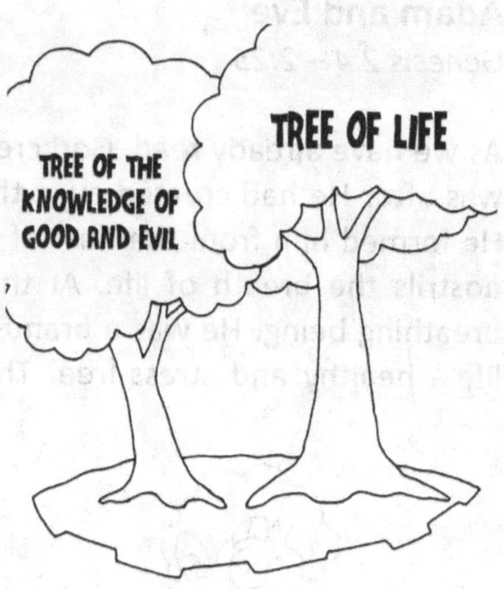

There was a river that watered the garden that flowed from Eden and it branched off into four headwaters, which were named:

Pishon
- Flowed through the entire land of Havilah.
- The area contained gold (which had a good smell to it) and onyx.

Gihon
- Flowed through the land of Cush.

Tigris
- It ran along the east side of Asshur.

Euphrates

God put this man in the Garden of Eden. His job was to work the land and take care of everything. It was a job, so he was expected to do something with his life. He didn't just sit around petting animals and eating fruit all day. He worked. It sounded like a simple task, but it came with a warning. God told him he could eat from every tree in the garden, except for one. He could not eat from the tree of the knowledge of good and evil. If he did, he would die. That's putting it out there in simple, easy-to-understand instructions. He gave the command and even gave the consequence ahead of time. If you had a thousand trees in front of you to eat from, ignoring that one tree should have been pretty easy to do. Wouldn't you think?

God didn't think it was a good idea for this man to be alone. He

felt like he needed a helper; someone or something that could work along with him, to talk with, to share ideas and thoughts with and to basically join together with to tackle this thing called 'life' with as a team. So, God brought all of the animals to Adam and told him to name each one. Adam named them. But, sadly for Adam, none of these animals filled that gap in his life as a helper and teammate.

Later, when Adam was asleep. God did something miraculous. He created for him a woman. To make her extra special for him, He used Adam's rib to make it

23

happen. She was made from him and for him. "Bone of my bones and flesh of my flesh." This is the example of how marriage should be. When a man leaves his father and mother to be united with his wife, the couple should spiritually become one. Everything we do and say from that point forward will affect the other. We need to be more thoughtful of our spouse because spiritually they are a part of us.

I know when my wife and I got married, the first few years took a little getting used to. Before marriage, we both worked independently and lived our life based on how we wanted to. But, because of this thing called 'marriage', we had to learn to consider each other's thoughts and feelings before we made any decisions and actions on our own. We had to learn that we were now a 'team' and that we tackled life together as one. If not, arguments would occur and we didn't like to fuss.

The last verse lets us know that Adam and his new woman partner were both naked and felt no shame. They were innocent and probably didn't think twice about walking around butt naked. There was nothing wrong with it. It was when they sinned that everything became awkward.

It reminds me of when my kids were little. If we had company over at the house, my kids may decide, on the spur of the moment, to strip their clothes off and run around the house naked. I mean, they were babies. It was no big deal. They were innocent and didn't know any better. If they had done this as teenagers, then it would have been a problem. They knew better.

I imagine God's creation knew no wrong. Everything was acceptable. Life must have been peaceful and great. Look at where we are now, something went wrong somewhere. But, what happened? We're fixing to find out.

The Fall Of Man
Genesis 3:1 – 3:24

The serpent was a tricky joker. At this point, we can only assume that this serpent was Satan. At the beginning of these verses, it seems that his mission was to deceive the woman by making her question what God had told them not to do.

"Did God really say not to eat from any tree in this garden?"

Eve, who wasn't named until verse 20 (Genesis 3:20), must have thought about his question to her. She probably had to look back and try to remember 'word for word' what God had said. There may have been some doubt to the exact words. But, she came through and said, "He said we couldn't eat from the tree in the middle of the garden... not even touch it. If we do, we will die."

Satan responded to her and said, "You won't die. Actually, God knows that if you eat it, you will be like Him. You will know the difference between good and evil."

Even though this is partially true. The way he said it made her feel like God was holding something 'good' from her. He made it seem like this tree was something special that only special people got to eat from. Eve probably forgot all of the great things He had done for them so far. Now she is questioning God's goodness and protection.

That's how Satan works. His plan against us is basically this:

Doubt - It makes us question God's Word and His goodness.

Discouragement – It makes us look at our problems instead of seeking God.

Diversion - It makes the wrong things seem attractive so that we will want them instead of the right things.

Defeat - It makes us feel like a failure to the point that we don't even want to try.

Delay - It makes us put off doing something so that it never gets done.

Eve walked over to the tree and saw that it was pleasurable to the eye and good enough to eat. So, she did. She took a bite and even gave Adam some. They next thing you know is that their eyes were opened and they became ashamed. They realized that they were naked and sewed up some fig leaves to cover themselves up. Their innocence was now gone.

When they heard the sound of God walking in the garden, they hid themselves from Him. They were afraid because of their nakedness. God realized quickly what had happened and began a series of curses to them and the serpent:

To the serpent
- Cursed above all the livestock and wild animals.
- Will crawl on his belly and eat dust all the days of his life.
- Enmity (true hatred) between the serpent and the woman and their offspring.
- "... it shall bruise thy head, and thou shalt bruise his heel." Genesis 3:15b. I think this refers to Satan's attacks on Jesus' ministry and how Jesus will prevail in the end.

To the woman
- Increased labor pains in childbearing.
- Her desire will be for her husband and he will rule over her.

A thought to ponder: Did labor pains not exist in the beginning of creation? Having babies with no pain? I bet women would have loved this idea.

To the man

- The ground will be cursed. He will have to work hard to 'just survive' all the days of his life.
- He was created with dust and to dust he will return (death).

A thought to ponder: Did man not have to work hard in the beginning? Was life all 'easy peasy lemon squeezy'? That would have been nice.

In Genesis 3: 20, Adam finally gives the woman a name. He calls her Eve because she would be 'the mother of all the living'. I just wonder why it took him so long to come up with a three-letter name.

God made clothing from skin to cover both Adam and Eve. He also banished them from the Garden of Eden. They weren't allowed to return. He placed cheribum (angels) and a flaming sword to guard the tree of life so that Adam and Eve could never touch it. That's a sad ending to what would have been a wonderful story. You won't hear about this tree of life again until Revelation (2:7, 22:2, 22:14). This is when humanity is offered an opportunity to eat from it and have eternal life.

The life we live today wasn't what the original plan started out to be. It was the sin of disobedience that changed everything – not only for Adam and Eve, but for the entire human race. Kinda makes you want to cry a little, doesn't it?

Cain and Abel
Genesis 4:1 – 4:26

Adam and Eve had relations like normal couples do. Birth control wasn't invented yet, so Eve got pregnant. Their first child was a boy. They named him Cain – no middle name or no last name. A simple first name was all that was needed back then. Later, she got pregnant again and had another son. This one they named Abel. That is pretty much all of the details that was given on this event. I don't think we needed to know any more than that. These verses go from conceiving two sons to what sounds like putting these children immediately to work in the fields. I'm sure years passed before their work began. But, then again, child labor laws weren't invented yet and maybe children started in the labor force the day they first began to walk. Surely not. Let's just hope they were in their teens.

Cain and Abel's job was to keep the flock and work the soil – basically taking care of animals and gardening. It says that both of them made offerings to God with what they had produced from their hard work. Cain offered some fruit from the soil and Abel offered the fat portions from the firstborn of his flock. It appears that God liked the offering that Abel gave and not so much on Cain's. This made Cain very angry. God told him to do what is right. If not, sin would be at his door because sin wanted him, but he had to master it.

I thought about this and think that maybe Cain did something wrong. Yes, he made an offering to God, but was it with true intentions? Was his motives in the right place? Did he keep the best fruit for himself and give God the rotted portions? Maybe. It's like that for the Christian today. We know that God wants us to do something for Him. This is our sacrifice to Him – to use the gift or talent that He gave us to use for His glory. What do we offer Him? Is it our best? Or do we sorta throw something together and hope that He will be pleased with it? Do we offer our sacrifice to God out of selfish gain? An example would be that of a singer. Are we truly singing praises to God or seeking the praises of man. I don't know.

Cain became jealous of Abel and schemed a plan to settle the score. He convinced him to go with him to the field. It was there that Cain chose to kill his brother. This is the first murder recorded in history. Abel died that day.

God knew what Cain had done and cursed him. No longer would his hard work yield crops. He would be a wanderer on the Earth. Sin had triumphed again and it came with a price. Cain felt that His punishment was too much. He would be removed from the land that he had known. Plus, he would be hidden from the presence of God. As a restless wanderer, he feared that someone would kill him.

Now, as we were reading up to this point, our brain was thinking that there were only four people living on Earth – Adam, Eve, Cain and Abel. And since Abel is dead, that would only leave three. Who would Cain fear? We don't really know how much time has passed up to Abel death. We learn later in Genesis, that people were living for long periods of time – almost 1000 years. There could have been a major population explosion within this time period.

God assured Cain that if anyone killed him, they would suffer vengeance seven times over. God put a mark on him so that no one who found him would kill him. Cain left the land that he was raised on and moved to live in the land of Nod which was east of Eden.

The next few verses seems to be a genealogy timeline for Cain. It breaks down like this:

Cain > Enoch > Irad > Mehujael > Methushael > Lamech

Lamech married two women: Adah and Zillah. He had children with both of them:

With Adah > Jabal and Jubal
Jabal was the father of those who live in tents and raise livestock. Jubal was the father of all who played harps and flutes.

With Zillah > Tubal-Cain and Naamah
Tubal-Cain was gifted with the talent of forging all kinds of tools out of bronze and iron.

I think the importance of knowing what these family members were good at is knowing that God provides talents, skills and abilities to everyone. We have to discover what that ability is and use it for God.

It seems that, in verses 23 and 24, sin had traveled its way down the genealogy pool and landed on Lamech. It appears that the sin that was committed by Cain had now been committed by Lamech in just five generations of time. But, why? Or, how?

I think it has to do with how our actions affect our kids. If we act sinful, chances are, our kids will learn from us and accept this lifestyle as something normal for themselves. They will, in turn, reflect it in the way they act and pass it down to their children. Keep in mind, we all have an opportunity to change. We can break those chains and decide not to act the way our fathers did. We can go our own path and start something new that is more positive and change the course of life for the whole gene pool. The main thing is taking that step to do something to change it.

The last two verses tells us that Adam and Eve were blessed by God with another child. They felt that this new child was a replacement gift for the one they lost (Abel). They named him Seth. Can you imagine what life was like for them? They had one child that was murdered and another child that was banished from home. Adam and Eve had a big void in their life. I can see why they considered Seth a blessing. Can't you?

The genealogy continued by stating that Seth had a child named Enosh in the last verse. Keep in mind, these names were probably popular back in the day even though they sound very strange now. Maybe they will come back in style. Who knows? Maybe your great great great grandson will name his son Enosh one day. That would be cool, wouldn't it? I don't know. Enosh sounds like one of them weird casseroles our aunts bring to our get-togethers at Thanksgiving.

"So, what dish did you bring for Thanksgiving this year, Aunt Bertha?"

"Well, honey, I brought your favorite... Enosh Casserole. Just make sure I get my Tupperware back."

Adam's Descendants: From Adam to Noah
Genesis 5:1 – 5:32

God created man – both male and female – in the likeness of Himself. He called his creation... man. As His creation started bearing offspring, they were created in the likeness of their parents, too. Genesis Chapter 5 seems to be all about the genealogy of Adam all the way down to Noah. It mentions how long each person lived. It tells us that these people also had other children, even though their names aren't mentioned. I'll try to break this down:

- Adam had a son named Seth at 130 years old and died at 930.
- Seth had a son named Enosh at 105 years old and died at 912.
- Enosh had a son named Kenan at 90 years old and died at 905.
- Kenan had a son named Mahalalel at 70 years old and died at 910.

- Mahalalel had a son named Jared at 65 years old and died at 895.
- Jared had a son named Enoch at 162 years old and died at 962.
- Enoch had a son named Methuselah at 65 years old and didn't die. It says that Enoch walked with God and was taken away.
- Methuselah had a son named Lamech at 187 years old and died at 969.
- Lamech had a son named Noah at 182 years old and died at 777.
- After Noah was 500 years old, he had sons: Shem, Ham and Japheth.

The Hebrew people kept good tracking records of their ancestors. They may have felt that these people were of great importance that needed to be shared with their descendants for many generations to come. I'm sure each of these people had a special story that needed to be shared. It could have been their story of faith that everyone could learn from.

I think what is cool about this list is the fact that they had kids at an old age and how long they lived their life. Is that even possible? The Bible says it, so it has to be true. How did they live so long? If I am showing signs of wrinkles at 50, can you imagine how wrinkly someone would be at 969

years old? My goodness! They would have looked liked the Cryptkeeper! But, maybe people didn't age as quickly back then. Their food was fresh and organic without chemicals and steroids. Maybe a 700 year old man was the equivalent of what a 30 year old looks like today. That would be interesting.

And what about the fact that Enoch didn't die. He had a kid at 65 and, all of a sudden, God took him. He just vanished! That's amazing. Where did he go? Let's also not forget the fact that Enoch's son holds the longest record of being the oldest man in history. He was 969 years old! Being 'old as Methuselah' is usually a term we use to describe someone we think of as being old, like in their 80's or something? To date, no one has defeated this record and I don't see this happening any time soon. But, 969 years old? Really? We're fortunate if we make it to 75. Right?

I imagine, back then, diseases weren't invented yet. Plus, God may have wanted to allow time for people to populate the Earth by giving them a longer lifespan.

The Story Of Noah

The Flood
Genesis 6:1 – 8:22

Hollywood has made big bucks off of telling this story through the years. I have seen a few of these movies for myself. I'll admit, many of them were kind of boring. The one made in 2004 starring Russell Crowe was pretty good with all of it's CGI effects, but they missed out on some of the facts from the Bible. But, at least they made an attempt to tell the story on the big screen. I read somewhere that the movie grossed 362 million dollars worldwide, which means it had a lot of viewers across the globe. That's a good thing. But, my favorite Noah-ish movie was Evan

Almighty that came out in 2007. It had a similar story line as what we read from the Bible. But, the message I received from the movie was that, by trusting God and His provision, He could change the world through us. And that's exactly what happened to Noah.

Whether from the movies, family members or from church, somewhere down the road someone has told us the story about the flood. The story is basically about a man named Noah, who was chosen by God, to build a boat that would save his family and two of every animal on the Earth from the destruction that God was about to bring to all of humanity. The world had become so evil and beyond repair. It would be Noah's family that would start humanity all over again from scratch. It would be a fresh new slate – a new starting point – for the world as we know it today. The end. Right?

Beginning in Genesis 6, we learn that the Earth was getting populated. We also learn that it wasn't a great place to live. Evil was everywhere. From what I have read in the first few verses, the root of the problem seems to be in the whole mating process. It says that 'the sons of God' were marrying beautiful women – any of them they chose – and having children. It mentions that 'the Nephilim' were on the Earth in those days, too. God wasn't too happy about the stuff that was going on and gave them 120 years to get their junk together. First of all, who were the 'sons of God'? Secondly, who or what is a 'Nephilim'? What was going on here?

Unfortunately, these questions are one of them debatable topics that have several possible answers.

The three main views on who the 'sons of God' are:

1. They were fallen angels.
2. They were powerful human rulers.
3. They were godly descendants of Seth intermarrying with wicked descendants of Cain.

What were the Nephilim? According to Hebraic and other legends, they were a race of giants (probably 9 to 10 feet tall) and super-heroes who did acts of great evil. Their great size and power likely came from the mixture of demonic 'DNA' with human genetics. All that the Bible directly says about them is that they were "heroes of old, men of renown" (Genesis 6:4). The Nephilim were not aliens or angels. They were literal, physical beings produced from the union of the sons of God and the daughters of men. They were one of the primary reasons for the great flood in Noah's time.

God wasn't too happy about how the people on Earth were acting. They were wicked and evil. His solution was to wipe them off the face of the Earth — including the animals, creatures and birds. Plain and simple.

Noah was favored by God. There was something special about him. God considered him righteous and blameless among the people. The Bible says that he walked with God.

God told Noah of His plan to rid the people of the Earth with a flood. He told Noah to build an ark (maybe a large boat) made of cypress wood with rooms in it. He said to make it airtight by coating it with 'pitch' (a tar-like coating) to keep the water out. It had to be made to specific dimensions: 450 feet long, 75 feet wide and 45 feet high. This wasn't an ordinary boat. It had a roof, a door on the side and three levels. I read that the ark was the length of one and a half football fields and as tall as a four-story building. This thing must have been huge!

God made a covenant with Noah and said that he could bring his wife, his sons (Shem, Ham and Japheth) and his sons' wives with him. This is where it gets difficult. God told him to gather up two of every living creature (male and female) – birds, crawly things and every kind of animal - and put them in the ark. He had to keep them alive – which means he had to feed them. I'm sure that wasn't an easy task. He had to bring enough food for them and his family to last during the entire heroic adventure.

In addition to these animals that he had to bring with him, he had to bring seven of every kind of clean animal (male and female) and two of every kind of unclean animal (male and female) – and keep them alive. That means more food! I think these animals were for ceremonial offerings to God that Noah would use at a later time.

Noah did everything that God commanded him to do – he built the ark, loaded the animals and stored the food. God told him to enter the ark and wait seven days. The flood was coming and it would last 40 days and 40 nights.

Here are some cool things that I found about this whole adventure:

- Noah was 600 years old when he built the ark.
- Scholars say, that based on the size of the ark, 45,000 animals could have fit inside.
- The Bible states that all the animals 'came to Noah'. That's a good thing because I imagine it would have been difficult trying to gather them himself. Have you ever tried to catch a chicken? It's not an easy task.
- The water flooded the Earth for 150 days.
- On the seventh day of the seventh month, the ark rested on top of the mountains of Ararat. This is located in the country of Turkey.
- On the first day of the tenth month, the water receded enough to see the mountain tops.
- After waiting an additional 40 days, Noah sent out a raven and a dove to see if the water had receded enough to see the ground. The dove returned because it didn't find any dry ground. Noah waited seven more days and sent the dove out again. This time, it returned with a freshly plucked olive leaf. Noah waited an additional seven days and sent the dove out again. This time it didn't return.
- On the first day of the first month of Noah's 601st year, the water had dried up on the Earth. It was on the twenty-seventh day of the second month that the Earth was completely dry. It was finally safe for Noah to come out of the ark.

So, how long did Noah actually stay in the ark during the flood? Most people believe it was for only 40 days and 40 nights. But, if you add it all up from the scriptures and do some scientific calculations, it totals up to be 378 days. That's a long time to be cramped up with a bunch of family members and stinky animals? Can you imagine taking a year-long road trip with your inlaws — cramped up together with all of their pets? Umm... I don't think so. This would have to go down in history as the worst road trip ever. But, at least Noah and his family were saved and blessed.

The first thing Noah did, when he got off the ark, was to build an altar to God. He gave burnt offerings from the clean animals and birds that God told him to bring. God also made a promise to never curse the ground again and destroy all living creatures with a flood and sealed this promise with a token in the sky – a rainbow.

I do set my bow in the cloud, and it shall be for a token of a covenant between me and the earth. And it shall come to pass, when I bring a cloud over the earth, that the bow shall be seen in the cloud: And I will remember my covenant, which is between me and you and every living creature of all flesh; and the waters shall no more become a flood to destroy all flesh. And the bow shall be in the cloud; and I will look upon it, that I may remember the everlasting covenant between God and every living creature of all flesh that is upon the earth. And God said unto Noah, This is the token of the covenant, which I have established between me and all flesh that is upon the earth. - Genesis 9: 13-17

Repopulating The Earth
Genesis 9:1 – 9:17

God blessed Noah and his sons. He told them to be fruitful and multiply. He wanted them to fill the Earth back up. Humans were now in short supply and it was up to Noah's family to get the ball rolling. If you look at our total population today (currently estimated at 7.7 billion people), according to the Bible, it began with Noah, his three sons and their wives. That's like 8 people. Wow!

Genesis 9: 3 starts a conversation about food. God is telling Noah that he can eat anything that lives and moves. Adam and Eve were given plants and now Noah begins the growing trend of being a meat-eater. That's great for many of us. I mean, salads are good, but there's something special about eating a delicious hamburger fresh off the grill. Know what I mean?

However, this freedom of being able to 'eat everything that moves' came with some accountability. For starters, God didn't want him to eat animal blood. It had to be drained. I imagine this had spiritual and physical significance to it. For example, blood was used for the atonement of sins. I guess eating it and using it for sacrifices sorta created a conflict of interest. Or, maybe God knew that raw animal blood could cause diseases in humans if consumed. Maybe He was just looking out for him. Lastly, I believe God wanted Noah to respect nature and only kill what he planned to eat. The opposite would be a hunter that killed animals just for the sport of it or just for the trophy deer

head to hang on his living room wall. Not that hanging a deer head on your wall is a bad thing. It's what you decide to do with the remaining 80% of the deer. You should probably eat it.

God also wanted Noah to be accountable for the life of his fellow man. Since God made man in His own image, murdering them would be a bad thing.

The Sons Of Noah
Genesis 9:18 – 9:29

The Bible tells us that four men came out of the ark – Noah, Shem, Ham and Japheth. Since Noah was good at working the soil like most farmers were, he decided to plant a vineyard. Noah used it to make some wine. He drank it and got drunk. He got so drunk that he passed out and fell asleep naked. Now, this is coming straight from the Bible. I'm not making this stuff up.

Noah, a man favored by God, gets drunk and passes out naked. There he is just laying all sprawled out butt-naked for everyone to see. Ham (father of Canaan), one of Noah's sons, was the first to see his Dad in this condition. The first thing he did was go tell his brothers about it. It was Shem and Japheth that walked in backwards with a garment and covered their Dad up. They even looked the other way so that they wouldn't see him in this naked drunken state. When Noah woke up, he was all upset. He put a curse on Ham and his descendants (Canaan).

At the same time, he blessed Shem and Japheth and their future families. OK. What just happened here?

It obvious that Noah got drunk. It's also known that Noah was passed out naked. Let's try and move on past that. I think the way his sons reacted towards the situation was the scene changer. Ham could have just covered him up and left it at that. But no, he had to get his brothers involved. It's almost like he wanted to embarrass his father. It could be to downgrade Noah's character to his family – to make him appear to be less than a man or something. This would have been very disrespectful to Noah. This action changed the course of their life and the life of their future generations. Ham's son, Canaan, and his bloodline would be slaves to his brothers (Shem and Japheth).

Noah lived an additional 350 years after the flood. He died at the ripe old age of 950 years old.

The Table Of Nations
Genesis 10:1 – 10:32

Here we go again with another genealogy. These can get boring, but they are needed. This one is of the sons of Noah and their descendants. I'll try and break it down for you:

A. Japheth (the Japhethites)
1. **Gomer**
- Askenaz
- Riphath
- Togarmah
2. **Magog**
3. **Madai**
4. **Javan**
- Elishah (the Kittam)

- Tarshish (the Rodanim)
5. **Tubal**
6. **Meshech**
7. **Tiras**

B. Ham (the Hamites)

1. **Cush**
   - Seba
   - Havilah
   - Sabtah
   - Raamah
     - Sheba
     - Dedan
   - Sabteca
   - Nimrod
2. **Mizraim**
   - Ludites
   - Anamites
   - Lehabites
   - Naphtuhites
   - Pathrusites
   - Casluhites (this where the Philistines came from)
   - Caphtorites
3. **Put**
4. **Canaan**
   - Sidon
   - Hittites
   - Jebusites
   - Amorites
   - Girgashites
   - Hivites
   - Arkites
   - Sinites
   - Arvadites
   - Zemarites
   - Hamathites

c. Shem (the Semites)

1. **Elam**
2. **Asshur**
3. **Arphaxad**
- Shelah
  - Eber
    * Peleg
    * Joktan
      ** Almodad
      ** Sheleph
      ** Hazarmaveth
      ** Jerah
      ** Hadoram
      ** Uzai
      ** Diklah
      ** Obal
      ** Abimael
      ** Sheba
      ** Ophir
      ** Havilah
      ** Jobab

4. **Lud**
5. **Aram**
- Uz
- Hul
- Gether
- Meshech

Here's something I found from my Study Bible about Bible Nations That Descended From Noah's Sons:

1. **Shem**
- Hebrews
- Chaldeans
- Assyrians
- Persians
- Syrians

47

2. **Ham**
*   Canaanites
*   Egyptians
*   Philistines
*   Hittites
*   Amorites
3. **Japheth**
*   Greeks
*   Thracians
*   Scythians

From the sons of Noah came different nations, territories, clans and different languages that was spread out all over the Earth after the flood. Since life as we know it came from Noah, the chances of us originating from one of these family members is pretty good. I just wouldn't know how to tell which one we originally came from. Would you?

The Tower Of Babel
Genesis 11:1 – 11:9

Back in the day, everyone had one language and a common speech. We have came a long way since then. There's all types of languages now. And what makes it even worse is that there are different varieties and styles of any certain language. To explain, just the language of English in my country can be spoken

in different ways. In the United States of America, if you live in the southern states - such as Alabama, Georgia and Tennessee – we have transformed it into what we consider Southern English. It's basically taking English words, adding a Southern drawl and either giving it an extra syllable or combining a group of words together and turning it into one. Or, we simply create new words all together. Here's a few examples:

English phrase: How are you doing?
Our version: How ya'll doin'?
Note: The Southern word **y'all** has became so popular that it has now been added to dictionaries, school curriculum and even the board game Scrabble. It's basically two words: **YOU** and **ALL** put together.

English words: Going to
Our version: Gonna

English words: Let me
Our version: Lem-me

English word: Teasing
Our version: Pickin'
Used in a sentence: Aww, come on now, aah'm (I'm) just pickin' wid (with) ya (you).

English word: Complain
Our version: Pitch a fit
Used in a sentence: Don't pitch a fit about that dray-ess (dress).

English phrase: Turn out the light.
Our version: Cut the light off
Used in a sentence: Cut the light off, Sugah.

English words: Getting ready to do something
Our version: Fixin'
Used in a sentence: Aah'm (I'm) fixin' to change that taar (tire).

English words: To figure or think
Our version: Reckon
Used in a sentence: Aah (I) reckon we kin (can) make it in time.

Our language is so confusing that it doesn't work well with the latest voice operated techno devices such as Amazon's Alexa. We should know because we own one. It seems every time I try to use it, it doesn't understand a single word I say. Maybe one day they'll create one just for the Southern English speaking people.

Another bad thing about our style of language is that, if we write books and spell our words in the books the way we say them, you cannot use online programs, such as Google Translate, to translate the books into other languages. I tried this one time earlier in one of my books. I wanted to create a German version and make it available for downloads in Germany. It seemed easy enough. All I had to do was copy/paste and press the 'translate' button. I would then copy/paste this translated version into the new book. No big deal. Right? Wrong. I started getting some negative feedback from the readers in Germany. I had to take the book down from the Internet. The translations were wrong and I looked like an idiot.

Here's another quick story. I was at a birthday party at my wife's best friend's house. I was trying to mingle with the people in attendance, so I sat at a table with three older ladies. They were having conversations, so I thought it would be cool for me to join in. I finally found an opportunity and started talking. The next thing I know is that, as I was talking, these three ladies are staring at my lips with a weird confused look on their faces. It was like they were struggling to understand what I was trying to say. Later that day I learned that they were from Boston.

Anyway, back to Genesis...

From Chapter 11, we learn that everyone spoke the same language and were moving eastward to a plain in Shinar. They decided they wanted to use man-made bricks and build them a city. They wanted to incorporate a large tower that reached the heavens. They thought, by doing so, they would make a name for themselves and not be scattered over the face of the Earth. They basically wanted to look like they had power and greatness with a huge monument for the world to see. They were focused on making themselves look good instead of channeling that energy on God.

God changed their plans by confusing their language so that they couldn't understand each other and scattered them all over the Earth. The building of the city stopped. That is why it was called Babel. That is how we have the many different languages that we have today – including Southern English.

Sometimes we build monuments to ourselves for others to see. It can be things such as expensive clothes, big house, fancy car and important job to draw attention to our achievements. These things can be good, but when we use them to give us identity and self-worth, they take God's place in our lives. What 'towers' have you built in your life?

From Shem To Abram
Genesis 11:10 – 11:32

More genealogy. I'll break it down:

- Shem – became the father of Arphaxad at 100 – he lived for an additional 500 years and had more kids.
- Arphaxad – became the father of Shelah at 35 – he lived for an additional 403 years and had more kids.
- Shelah – became the father of Eber at 30 – he lived for an additional 403 years and had more kids.
- Eber – became the father of Peleg at 34 – he lived for an additional 430 years and had more kids.
- Peleg – became the father of Reu at 30 – he lived for an additional 209 years and had more kids.
- Reu – became the father of Serug at 32 – he lived for an additional 207 years and had more kids.
- Serug – became the father of Nahor at 30 – he lived for an additional 200 years and had more kids.
- Nahor – became the father of Terah at 29 – he lived for an additional 119 years and had more kids.
- Shem – became the father of Arphaxad at 100 – he lived for an additional 500 years and had more kids.
- Terah – became the father of Abram, Nahor and Haran at 70.

This is the accounts of Terah:

- Terah became the father of Abram, Nahor and Haran.
- Haran became the father of Lot.
- Haran died in his hometown of Ur while his father, Terah, was still alive.
- Abram married Sarai.
- Nahor married Milcah (which was one of his brother Haran's daughters).
- Sarai was barren and had no children.
- Terah took Abram (his son), Lot (his grandson) and Sarai (his daughter-inlaw) and moved out of Ur to Canaan. They settled in Haran.
- Terah lived an additional 205 years and died in Haran.

Some of the interesting things to me from reading this are:

1. Either Terah took on the responsibility of being a father to his grandson, Lot, or
2. Abram chose to be the father of his brother's son, Lot, which is great because his wife couldn't have children.
3. Terah, Abram, Sarai and Lot moved to a place that shared the same name as the deceased brother/son/father (Haran).

The Story Of Abraham

God Promises A Nation To Abram
Genesis 12:1 – 12:9

Abram was a man that God chose to build a great nation. Abram's instructions were to leave Ur – the place where his friends and family lived. He took his wife, Sarai, his adopted son (Lot), his people (maybe slaves) and material possessions. So, out of faith, he did as God instructed. From his obedience, God promised him blessings and that he would also be a blessing to others. Abram's future looked promising. God was giving him new land to start something new that would impact his generations to come. Would you leave everything you know to go where God wanted you to be?

Abram traveled onward. It seems like every time he would stop or set up his tent, he would always build an altar to God. Altars back in those days were used to make sacrifices and were usually made from piled up stones. It is where God's people made communion with Him. It was also used as a place to pray, worship and renew their love and loyalty with God. The great thing about altars made from stone, is that people usually didn't take them down when they were finished using them. I'm sure there were many of them just lying around somewhere. If a person saw one, they would know what they were used for. It would be a reminder to God's people that maybe they should build one for themselves and get reconnected back to God. And for the person that came across an old altar that they had built years ago, it would remind them of that special day that they reached out to God – and God reached back and answered their prayers.

That would be a great purpose for keeping a Prayer Journal. Not only can you pray effectively by listing things you want to pray about, but you can always look back on it to remember everything you've prayed about and thank God for answering them. I mean, we pray for stuff now and usually forget about it. Wouldn't it be cool to see God work with the use of a Prayer Journal? I think so.

Abram In Egypt
Genesis 12:10 – 12:20

Abram was seventy five years old when he began his God-called traveling adventure. He took his family and stopped at various places along the way. In these verses, it seems that there was a severe famine where he currently resided and he was forced to go down to Egypt. I can only assume that maybe Egypt had more resources available that would keep Abram and his family alive.

Before they reached Egypt, Abram had a fearful thought. He felt that the Egyptians would kill him. Polygamy (having multiple wives) was legal in Egypt and practiced by those in royalty. A pharaoh would have his royal wife and he would also have other wives, too. Since Abram knew how beautiful his wife (Sarai) was, he knew that she would be chosen by Pharaoh as soon as he laid eyes on her. Of course, he would have to kill her husband first. Abram didn't want that to happen. So, he came up with a plan.

He tells Sarai to tell everyone that she was his sister. This would save his life and give him bonus points for being a brother of such a beautiful lady. Yes, it was a lie – but, not a complete lie. We will learn later that in Genesis 20:12 that Sarai was actually Abram's half-sister. They shared the same father.

And yet indeed she is my sister; she is the daughter of my father, but not the daughter of my mother; and she became my wife. - Genesis 20: 12

OK, let's stop right here. I wish we could just move on past this 'being married to his half-sister' topic and pretend we didn't read it. I mean, it's not something you would expect to read about in the Bible. Being married to a relative or anyone that is close to being related to us is usually frowned upon in our culture today. It's just something we don't do.

One of the first things I have always practiced when my oldest kids were dating was to ask them questions about their latest boyfriends and girlfriends. I wanted to know their last names. Then, I would ask who their parents were. I needed last names and maiden names. For their safety, I would try and make sure that there were no possible links in being related to these people. I didn't want my kids dating potential cousins. My family ancestry tree is huge and many of these people never moved from where we live now. There was a chance that my kid would one day fall in love with someone that they were related to. This would make it awkward at family reunions. Plus, their future kids could grow to have a genetic malfunction or something. It was for their own good and they finally got tired of me asking questions.

But, what was the deal with Abram being married to his half-sister? Wasn't it against the law?

And if a man shall take his sister, his father's daughter, or his mother's daughter, and see her nakedness, and she see his nakedness; it is

a wicked thing; and they shall be cut off in the sight of their people: he hath uncovered his sister's nakedness; he shall bear his iniquity. - Leviticus 20: 17

From what I've read, the law didn't come into effect until way after Abram and Sarai were married. Plus, it was believed that it was customary for families to maintain their bloodline by intermarrying with relatives. I guess, at the time, they didn't see anything wrong with it. It was when the laws were presented to the people by Moses that everything changed. Anyway, back to the scriptures.

Just as Abram hoped, he and his family received special treatment. It says that he received sheep, cattle, male and female donkeys, menservants, maidservants and camels. Not too shabby of a deal for Abram.

God inflicted serious diseases on Pharaoh and his household because of Sarai. I guess this was a punishment to Pharaoh for his lustful desires. Pharaoh did the math and soon realized that the cause for these plagues were because of Abram's deceit. Instead of killing him, he allowed Abram to keep all of these riches and sent him and his family on their way.

What really happened here? It started with a famine. Abram goes to Egypt for survival, he meets up with Pharaoh (a wealthy man of royalty), Abram half-lies, Abram gets the royal treatment and it ends by Abram getting plenty of supplies to provide for his needs to last the journey to the land that God promised him. So this story is really about God's protection and provision. I thought that was pretty cool.

Abram and Lot

Genesis 13:1 – 13:18

Abram and his family (plus, everything he had – which was plenty) traveled from Egypt back to the place where he built his first altar to God. The scripture says that he was wealthy in livestock, silver and gold. Actually, between Abram and Lot, they had so much stuff that the land they lived on couldn't hold it all. This was causing arguments. Abram had to think quick.

He came up with a brilliant plan. It was time for them to go separate ways. Abram moved on to Canaan, while Lot chose to move to a place near Sodom. Unfortunately, the place where Lot was moving to was full of wicked people and they were happily sinning against God. This couldn't be good for the community and the people that lived there – including Lot. But, Lot didn't care. He was greedy and wanted the best land available, even if it was near all of that sin.

That's how it is in life. When we stop making choices in God's direction, our only option is to make choices in the wrong direction. Let that sink in for a minute.

Before Abram and Lot parted ways, God gave Abram some insight. He told him to look as far as he could, in all directions, across the land. This would be the land that God would give him and his offspring.

And to give Abram an idea of how many people would be included in his offspring, God mentioned that it would be like 'counting dust'. Dust is one of those things that's sorta 'uncountable'. So, based on this info, Abram was about to get blessed with a lot of kids. This would definitely be a miracle considering Abram and Sarai couldn't have any. But, hey. God always makes the impossible... possible. Right?

Abram Rescues Lot
Genesis 14:1 – 14:24

A war broke out. Cities were fighting against cities as an act of rebellion.

Team 1:
Amraphel (king of Shinar)
Arioch (king of Ellasar)
Kedorlaomer (king of Elam)
Tidal (king of Goiim)

Team 2:
Bera (king of Sodom)
Birsha (king of Gomorrah)
Shinab (king of Admah)
Shemeber (king of Zeboiim)
Zoar (king of Bela)

It seems that Team 2 had been ruled by the king from Team 1 (Kedorlaomer) for twelve years. They rebelled in the thirteenth year – probably by withholding tribute (maybe they stopped paying taxes or something). And on the fourteenth year, they went to war - four kings against five. In those days, the winner of a war took their opponents possessions. In this case, King Kedorlaomer, and the three kings that allied with him, won the war. The Bible says they took the possessions of Sodom and Gomorrah. This included their goods, food and even Abram's nephew, Lot (just because he just so happened to live there).

Lot's greedy desire to have the best of everything put him into sinful surroundings. And now he had become a prisoner. In the same way, we can be enticed into doing things or going places we shouldn't. We can become prisoners to it if our motives are not in line with God's desires.

Abram got word from a 'war escapee' that his nephew had become a prisoner, so he called out to 318 trained men born in his household to go get him. This wasn't just a normal 'prison break'. Oh no! This was another war between a mere 318 soldiers against four kings and their military personnel. Guess who won? Yep. Abram's men won the battle and took back Lot, his people and his possessions.

I guess everyone was amazed at this victory that the king of Sodom (Bera) wanted to meet with Abram. Melchizedek (the priest of God Most High) brought the bread and wine and blessed Abram by saying:

Blessed be Abram of the most high God, possessor of heaven and earth: And blessed be the most high God, which hath delivered thine enemies into thy hand. - Genesis 14: 19,20

Abram gave the king (Bera) a tenth of everything he had won through the battle. The king declined the offer and told Abram that he only wanted the people and that he could keep all of the goods. Abram didn't want any of it. He didn't want to feel like he was indebted to the king, nor wanted the king to feel like he was the reason for Abram's wealth. I think Abram wanted God to get the glory for all of his accomplishments. So, the only reward Abram received that day was the return of his nephew, Lot. That's all he ever really wanted anyway.

God Promises A Son To Abram
Genesis 15:1 – 15:21

Abram had just won a great battle. He may have had some fear to overcome him. Maybe he thought that the kings that he just defeated would try and seek revenge. Maybe Abram was feeling like he had made a bad decision by not taking all of the possessions that he had won in battle. It really doesn't say.

The beginning verses says that the Lord appeared to Abram in a vision and basically tells him, "Don't be afraid. I am your shield and your very great reward." Maybe Abram needed some comfort and reassurance.

All that we know is that Abram was thinking of the future. He may of thought about all that God had promised to him and his future generations to come. It sounded good and all, but there was this little problem. Abram and Sarai couldn't have kids. How can you create generations of people without being able to have a child? God reminded him of his promise and Abram believed Him. This is why Abram is known for being 'righteous'. It's because of his trust and belief in God when things didn't look so promising.

Abram needed assurance and guidance from God. He had questions and that's normal. God was giving Abram land and was going to build a nation on it.

"How can I know that I will gain possession of it?" Abram asked.

Keep in mind, the land that God was giving him was already occupied with people living there. This wasn't some kind of undiscovered island somewhere. People already owned this place. So, Abram made a very good point with his question.

God's response was for Abram to make a sacrifice to Him —
something very specific. He
was to sacrifice a heifer, a
goat and a ram and they
had to be three years old.
God also wanted a dove and
a young pigeon. I imagine
making a sacrifice like this
with its specific attention to
details would keep a
person's focus on God. Plus,
I'm sure it took some effort
in trying to locate animals
that were three years old.
What would you look for to
determine their age? I read
that this can be done by
counting their teeth. If

that's the case, then Abram probably went around opening up a
lot of animals' mouths and looking at their teeth. There's no
telling how many times he may have gotten bitten. After Abram
made this sacrifice, he fell into a deep sleep. That is when God
spoke to him.

*And he said unto Abram, Know of a surety that thy seed shall be
a stranger in a land that is not theirs, and shall serve them; and
they shall afflict them four hundred years; And also that nation,
whom they shall serve, will I judge: and afterward shall they
come out with great substance. And thou shalt go to thy fathers
in peace; thou shalt be buried in a good old age. But in the fourth
generation they shall come hither again: for the iniquity of the
Amorites is not yet full. - Genesis 15: 13-16*

Yes, his generations would possess the land that God promised him. However, at first, they will be strangers in this new land. They will serve the current owners of the land (Amorites) as slaves. The current owners will make it rough on them for four hundred years. But, after God judges them, Abram's descendants will come out of it with great riches. Abram will live a peaceful life and will die at a good old age.

It sounds like Abram's fourth generation would receive this promised land because God was giving the Amorites time to repent (and they never did). Abram would have to be patient and wait. And no one likes to wait, right?

On that day God made a covenant with Abram. He promised to give Abram's descendants the land, from the river of Egypt to the the great river Euphrates – the land of the Kenites, Kenizzites, Kadmonites, Hittites, Perizzites, Rephaites, Amorites, Canaanites, Girgashites and Jebusites. That's a lot of 'ites'!

Hagar and Ishmael
Genesis 16:1 – 16:16

Sarai, Abram's wife, was well aware of the promise that God made to them. She knew that He promised them children, but she must have grown impatient and got tired of waiting. She took it upon herself to 'make it happen' through her maidservant, Hagar.

Its almost like she thought, "If God isn't going to hold up to his promises, I will get a child somehow... someway."

I'm sure many of us are guilty of this, too. We pray for something and expect a quick response. We may be willing to wait a little while, but not too long. I believe sometimes God makes us wait on purpose. It's like He tests our patience and our faith. It's usually through our 'waiting time' that reveals our true heart. Do we truly trust Him to answer? We will know for sure by the 'thought battles' that may go on inside our head:

"It's been a while since I prayed. God hasn't answered... yet. But, I know He will. He has always answered my prayers in the past. This one is no different. Let His will be done in my life."

"Uggh! I've waited a week for God to answer my prayer. Does He really care?"

"God isn't going to answer. He doesn't even listen to me. I'll just go and make it happen my self!"

I imagine this is what happened to Sarai. She found her own solution instead of waiting on God. She makes Hagar sleep with her husband. And then, after Hagar gets pregnant, Sarai gets mad about it and starts blaming Abram for what had happened.

She also starts mistreating Hagar, which causes Hagar to skip town - leaving that 'psycho' behind. A mistake had been made, but Sarai didn't want to take responsibility for it. She didn't want to wait on God to fulfill His promise. It was easier for her to blame everyone else for her problem that she created.

The scene changes and Hagar is hanging out near a spring in the desert. An angel of the Lord appears to her and tells her to go back and make amends with Sarai. That's nice. Maybe they can work out their differences. He also gives her the news that her descendants will be increased so much that she won't be able to count them. That's a good thing. Everybody would like a big growing family one day – a family tree with a bunch of branches would be a great thing. The chilling news came when the angel said:

Behold, thou art with child, and shalt bear a son, and shalt call his name Ishmael; because the LORD hath heard thy affliction. And he will be a wild man; his hand will be against every man, and every man's hand against him; and he shall dwell in the presence of all his brethren. - Genesis 16: 11,12

At first, I thought this angel was going to give her some good news. Maybe he saw that she was stressed out and was going to give her calm words of encouragement. But, it sounds like he was giving her a warning about the child she was carrying in her womb. This was going to be a wild child – a trouble maker, a scoundrel – and it sounds like no one is going to like him. That can't be good. But, at least the baby received its new name – Ishmael. Maybe he won't be made fun of in school because of it.

Nine months passed (I assume) and Hagar had the baby. Abram, who was now eighty six years old when the child was born, named him Ishmael. I hope they enjoyed the early years of his birth because it doesn't seem like the future will be too bright for poor Ishmael. We'll see.

The Covenant Of Circumcision
Genesis 17:1 – 17:27

Abram was 99 years old. His wife, Sarai, was around 90 and their adopted son, Ishmael, was 13 according to the scriptures. It's kind of a strange family setting – two old folks trying to raise a teenager. Maybe the older people back then had more energy and patience. I don't think that would be a wise idea these days. But, somehow, they managed.

God was still promising Abram that He would bless him with the land of Canaan, even though they were currently being considered strangers while they stayed there. God was also going to bless him with a bunch of family members, even though he and Sarai couldn't bear children. Actually, God was so serious about all of this that He changed their names to reflect this promise. Abram would now be called Abraham (because the name Abraham means 'father of many') and Sarai's name would drop the 'i' and add the 'h' (because Sarah probably means something like 'mother of nations'). When God promised these great things, Abraham fell face down in honor to God, while at the same time, he laughed to himself. I think he saw the idea of being 100 years old (and Sarah being 90) with a child as an impossibility. He may of felt like God's timing was way off – it was too late for all of that. But, God thought otherwise and was still going to fulfill His promise.

God made another covenant with Abraham – which included all of his male offspring, male slaves and any fella that was part of Abraham's clan. God wanted them all to be circumcised. This included all men that were living that day and any men born in the future. All male babies at the age of eight days old will be circumcised. If they don't, they will be separated from their people. This wouldn't be a good thing.

Circumcision was a serious thing in the days of Abraham. It's what told the world that you belonged to Abraham's family tree and his household. Can you imagine how the menfolk shared this information with others?
Imagine this:

Two men are working at a job site (maybe they're painters) and they are having a conversation.

"Hi. My name is Steve and I'm part of the Hooba Looba clan from the South."

"Nice to meet you, Steve. My name is Harvey and I'm from the clan of Abraham from the East."

"The Abraham clan? Really?
You don't look like you're part of that clan. Your hair is blonde and your eyes are blue."

"Well, I am and I can prove it." (He unzips his pants)

In today's world, circumcision is a common thing to do to newborn baby boys. I think parents do it because of a hygiene thing and probably don't know where the whole concept originated. But, here you have it. Right here.

I remember back when my son was born about 29 years ago. He had popped out of the womb-chute and the nurses were cleaning him up. He was all gooey and gross. They wrapped him up in a hospital baby blanket and carried him off to another room. As the 'good Dad' that I wanted to be, I followed along with them to this room where we met up with a doctor holding a pair of scissors. He laid my son on a table and unfolded the blanket. He grabbed his taddy-whacker and began trimming skin off from around it. My son screamed and I was in total shock. I guess, for a brief moment, I thought they were cutting it off to turn my newborn son into a girl, but everything was still there. This was my first encounter with the circumcision process. The thought of it is still in my mind.

God included Ishmael in His blessing (because of Abraham's request). Ishmael would be blessed with a great nation and would be the father of twelve rulers. The future just got brighter for Ishmael.

The verses end with Abraham and all of his male household dwellers gathered together — doing normal guy stuff, you know, like getting all circumcised and junk. I imagine there were a lot of screaming men walking around in pain that day. But, they were just doing what God told them to do. That's all that matters.

The Three Visitors

Genesis 18:1 – 18:15

Abraham was just chilling at the doorway of his tent. He was in the shade of the great trees of Mamre. Scholars say that these were oak trees. In the South, where I am from, oak trees can get pretty huge. Maybe Abraham found shelter from the scorching heat by relaxing under these trees. It is also the place where the Lord appeared to him.

Abraham looked up and saw three men standing right there in front of him. He was so excited about it that he rushed down there to meet them. He was very hospitable. He offered them water for a relaxing foot bath and some prime select food. In today's world, this would be like getting a fine meal and a spa treatment. These three men were treated as royalty by Abraham.

It seems that the purpose of their visit was to inform Abraham and his wife, Sarah, that by this time next year, they would be the proud parents of a son. But, they had already known this. Why did they need to be reminded of this promise? And why did three men of God need to tell them?

Sarah's response is what really stood out to me from these verses. She laughed. It's almost like she forgot the fact that God promised her and Abraham a son. They pretty much just carried on with life and the thought of this promise never crossed their minds. They were up in age and life for them was 'made in the shade'. She may of felt that she was too old for kids and, at this point in her life, it really didn't matter if she had a child or not.

It's almost like when we pray for something and God doesn't answer right away. We carry on and learn to adapt without the answered prayer. We've given up on it and don't think about it anymore. If someone were to walk up to us and tell us that we are going to get that answer we prayed for, we would probably laugh and think, "What's the point? It's too late. We will be fine with or without it. It doesn't really matter anymore."

God's message to her is that 'nothing is impossible for Him'. He can do the impossible. It's also a message that tells us to not give up on what we ask for in prayer. If it seems that God isn't going to answer our prayer, we need to know that God hears us and his answers are given in His timing – not ours. We don't need to give up. Keep on praying and holding on to His promises.

Abraham Pleads For Sodom
Genesis 18:16 – 18:33

The cities of Sodom and Gomorrah had became sinful places. God wasn't too happy about it. God was fixing to destroy them from the face of the Earth. God shared His plans with Abraham.

The thought of this touched Abraham's heart. Abraham may have seen the bad stuff that was going on in Sodom and Gomorrah, but he also felt like there was something good there, too. So, he began pleading and negotiating with God to spare the people that lived there. The final result was that if Abraham could find at least ten righteous people living in those cities, He would spare everyone's life. He wouldn't destroy them.

If you think about the country, or even the city we live in, would you consider it a righteous place to live? Probably not. If we based the way everyone around us lives against the standards that God has for us, how would we rank on the righteous scale? Would it be grounds for a total annihilation by God? But, what if God's mercy on us was because of a few righteous people that lived here? Maybe they are pleading to God on our behalf. That's the scenario here in these verses. God hears the prayers of the righteous.

Sodom and Gomorrah Destroyed
Genesis 19:1 – 19:29

Lot was at the entrance gate of Sodom when the two angels arrived. If we remember back, Lot was the son of Haran (Abraham's dead brother). It seems that Lot was now living in Sodom, and because he was at the entrance gate, could've meant that he had a position in their government or knew someone that did. He may have been an important figure in that town. He also may have known how sinful his town had became because, in verse 2, it sounded like Lot was trying to rush these angels away or detour them from seeing how bad it really was.

Lot convinces them to stay at his house. He offers them food and rest. But, before they could go to bed for the night, Lot's house becomes surrounded by men – both young and old – from every part of the city. It was an ambush.

The men call out to Lot. In a weird chain of events, they request Lot to bring the two angels (in man form) out to them. Disturbingly, they wanted to have sex with them. OK. This just got really weird.

Lot steps outside to talk to this perverted mob that surrounded his house. He warns them to not do this 'wicked thing' that they are wanting to do. Instead, Lot offers them his daughters (who are already engaged). OK. It just got even weirder.

This place must have been really saturated in 'nasty' for a man to throw his daughters into the front line of a mob of sexual perverts. There is definitely something wrong going on here. Had this become the normal way of life for them?

At this point, the mob is about ready to break down Lot's front door. Luckily, the two angels pulled Lot back inside his house and struck the men outside the door with blindness. The angels inform Lot of what their purpose is for being there. Basically,:

"We're here to destroy the city because of all of the sin. Also, we are here to spare the lives of you and your family. Pack 'em up and get out of here!"

Lot hesitated. His son-inlaw didn't take the warning seriously. It's almost like no one wanted to leave. But, because of God's mercy, one of the angels grabs the hands of Lot, Lot's wife and their two daughters and leads them outside of the city. He tells them to run for their lives – run to the mountains and don't look back.

Instead of running to the mountains, Lot negotiated with the angels and was allowed to settle in a small town called Zoar. As soon as the sun had risen over the land, the destruction began. Burning sulfur rained down from the heavens on Sodom and Gomorrah. This wiped out the cities – including the people and vegetation. Lot's wife didn't listen to the angels warning. She thought it would be cool to turn around one last time and take a quick glance at the burning cities. When she did, she was transformed into a pillar of salt. The only survivors from this massive destruction were Lot and his two daughters.

A pillar of salt? When we think of salt, we think of how it makes food taste better. It offers flavor. It also acts as a preservative to help make food last longer. The guys from the old days would smear it all over raw meat and store the meat in a shed. For some reason the meat wouldn't decompose and the flies would stay away from it. When it came time to cook the meat, they would wash it off and fry it up. The salt preserved it.

Maybe there's some symbolism in the story of how Lot's wife became a pillar of salt. Sodom and Gomorrah was a sinful place. It could be that Lot's wife enjoyed her lifestyle living there. Maybe she really didn't want to leave. She turned around for one more last memory of the place she loved. Here's some scripture from Luke:

Remember Lot's wife. Whosoever shall seek to save his life shall lose it; and whosoever shall lose his life shall preserve it. - Luke 17: 32,33

There is pleasure in sin, but sin leads to death. We have to turn from it – walk away and don't look back – if we want to truly live.

Lot and His Daughters
Genesis 19:30 – 19:38

I have been reading some weird stuff so far in the Book of Genesis. Most of it has came from Chapter 19. First, we hear about grown men wanting to have sex with angels. Second, Lot offers his two daughters sexually to a mob of strange men. Now, we are reading about Lot's daughters taking advantage of their father by getting him drunk and having sex with him. We're talking about full-blown incest here and it's in the Bible. Wow!

Lot's daughters were afraid that they would never be able to marry and have children to carry on the family name. They took matters into their own hands and made it happen.

The older daughter had a son named Moab (who is the father of the Moabites). The younger daughter had a son named Ben-Ammi (who is the father of the Ammonites). The interesting thing to me is that these were two great nations that became enemies of Israel. Israel never conquered them and Moses was forbidden to attack them (Deuteronomy 2:9) because of the family connection. So, basically, the consequence of the sin of the two daughters created enemies of Israel that could never be conquered.

Overall, it seems that Lot and his family were carrying some sinful ways with them as they left Sodom and Gomorrah. It will probably infect its way into their generations to come. I'm sure of it.

Abraham and Abimelech
Genesis 20:1 – 20:18

I guess back in the day, if a married couple entered into a new land and the bride was an attractive lady, the royalty figure from the town could kill the husband and take the bride as his own. Abraham and Sarah must have known about this beforehand as they traveled because they created a plan that would save them on their journey. Abraham and Sarah would tell folks that they were

brother and sister, which wasn't a big lie because they were actually siblings but with different mothers.

Abraham and Sarah traveled to the region of Negev and stayed in Gerar (an area between Kadesh and Shur). They shared the scheme of telling everyone they were related. Abimelech, the king of Gerar, saw Sarah and wanted her for his own, so he sent for her.

OK. Keep in mind, Sarah was like 90. She must have been 'smoking hot' for the king to want her as his own. Or maybe he just liked older and more distinguished women. Hey. Whatever rocks his boat. You know? Anyway, back to the story...

God came to Abimelech in a dream one night and said, "You're a dead man because the woman you took is a married woman." I guess there was a conversation going on in the dream between God and Abimelech. If I had to put it into today's language, it would sorta sound like this:

"You're gonna die because you're messing with a married woman."

"Look. You wouldn't destroy a nation because of this, would you? Her brother told me that she was his sister. And the woman agreed. I didn't know the truth. It's not my fault."

"I know you didn't know. That's why I kept you from sinning against me by not letting you touch her. Now return the woman back to her husband. He's a good prophet fella and will pray for you – and you will live. If you don't return her, you can count on this... you and yours will die."

The next morning, Abimelech talks it over with his officials about what had happened to him. They became scared because this little event almost created the wrath of God on their nation. Later, they confront Abraham about what he had done to them and wanted to know why. Abraham's response was that he was afraid that he would be killed. I guess they all came to terms in the end because the next thing that happened was that Abimelech showers him with sheep, cattle, male and female slaves, a thousand shekels of silver and his choice of anywhere he wanted to live on his land. This could've turned out to be a very bad ending for either Abraham or Abimelech.

As an added bonus to this story, God heals Abimelech, his wife and his slave girls so that they could have children again. It says that God closed up every womb in Abimelech's household because of this little event with Sarah. God was serious about it.

What can we learn from all of this? The one thing that comes to mind is that of God's mercy. He protected Abimelech from sinning against Him unknowingly. He stopped things from happening that should have happened. Also, because of the way the chain of events happened, Abimelech may have learned to respect and fear Abraham's God. Sometimes we don't reach out to Him or learn more about Him until something drastic happens in our life. Maybe that's all Abimelech needed.

The Birth of Isaac
Genesis 21:1 – 21:7

The Lord finally fulfilled His promise to Abraham and Sarah. She became pregnant and delivered a son at the exact time God said they would. Abraham named him Isaac. And when Isaac was eight days old, he got circumcised.

Back in the day, having a child was considered a blessing and a gift from God. It was also looked upon by the people around them as a sign of being in good standing with God. I imagine Abraham and Sarah had felt sociably awkward in public for so many years for not having any children. But, this day was a great day for them. They could now hold their heads up high and be proud to be officially called 'parents' – even if Abraham was 100 years old.

Hagar and Ishmael Sent Away
Genesis 21:8 – 21:21

If we remember back, Hagar was the maidservant that Sarah used to give birth to a son for Abraham. Sarah couldn't wait for God's promise to her, so she took matters into her own hands and gave Abraham a son through Hagar. Ishmael was the offspring created by Abraham and Hagar.

From these verses, we see that God's promise to Sarah was fulfilled. She now had a son named Isaac. Isaac had grown in age. Actually, the Bible says he was weaned and they were throwing a great feast to celebrate this new stage in his life. From what I read, the age of a weaned child is anywhere between 18 months to 4 years old. So, I assume Isaac was somewhere in between.

Abraham put a feast together and two of the people in attendance were Hagar and Ishmael. It seems that Ishmael was mocking Isaac and this got Sarah upset. I also think she was a little bit jealous of the arrangements. She tells Abraham to get rid of Hagar and her son, Ishmael. She didn't want him to ever share in the inheritance with their son, Isaac. Out of sight , out of mind. Problem solved. Right?

Abraham was a good man. Despite the feelings of Sarah, he loved his son, Ishmael. Actually, in a few chapters back, he asked God to bless him. Because of Sarah's feelings about him, Abraham got a little stressed out about the whole situation. God told him to listen to Sarah and reassured him that he didn't need to worry because both sons would grow up to do great things.

The next morning, Abraham gives Hagar some food and water and sends her and Ishmael off to the desert in Beersheba. I imagine the weather was hot and dry because they ran out of water. At this point, they may have feared death. Hagar puts her son under a bush to shade him from the sun while she sat nearby in tears.

An angel of the Lord hears Ishmael crying and calls out to Hagar. He tells her to not be afraid and to take her son by the hand. He informed her that her son would one day be a great nation. And when God opened her eyes, she saw a well of water. They quenched their thirst and realized God saved them that day.

In the last verse, we learn that God was with the boy as he grew up. He was raised by his mother without an earthly dad. It's sad, but I have always heard that God would be a father to the fatherless.:

A father of the fatherless, and a judge of the widows, is God in his holy habitation. - Psalm 68:5

Maybe Ishmael's childhood wasn't as bad as we would imagine, especially when God was in it. It says he lived in the desert and became an archer. This is someone that shoots with a bow and arrow. Maybe he learned a trade or at least learned how to get his own food for survival.

The verses end with Hagar getting her son a wife from Egypt and saying that they lived in the Desert of Paran. Sounds like a good ending to a story considering it could've stopped that day when they ran out of water in the desert. They could have died, but God was with them.

The Treaty At Beersheba
Genesis 22:22 – 22:34

King Abimelech and his commander, Phicol, tells Abraham, "God is with you in everything you do. Swear to me here before God that you will not deal falsely with me, my children or my descendants. Show kindness to me and the country you are living in as an alien – the same kindness as I've shown you."

Abraham replies, "I swear it."

I guess Abraham got a bad wrap for his half-lies to Abimelech a few verses back. It almost cost the king his life and could have destroyed his nation. From now on, he wanted to hear the truth. He was so serious about it that he made Abraham 'swear' to it. He wanted to make this deal 'of truth' to include his future generations, too. He was that serious.

After this agreement between them, Abraham presented his first complaint to the king. He was questioning the ownership of a well that was seized by one of the king's servants. The king didn't know anything about it. This was the first time that he had even heard about this. So, Abraham brought sheep and cattle to the king and they made a treaty. Out of the sheep that he brought, Abraham presented seven female sheep as a witness that he dug the well. I guess this means that he wanted the king to allow him to own it. The king agreed. The place that these two men swore an oath was called Beersheba.

The last verses tell us that Abraham planted a tamarisk tree there in Beersheba and stayed in the land of the Philistines for a long time.

What was the importance of planting the tamarisk tree? Was this a special kind of tree? The Bible doesn't really say, There are some speculations. Some folks think that maybe, since Abraham was going to live there a long time, he wanted the place to look like the environment that he had grown up in. Maybe he wanted it feel more like home. I read that tamarisk trees take a long time to grow, so I'm not sure if Abraham would have benefited from it. Maybe he just wanted to leave a landmark (a reminder) for his future generations to see that would remind them of the oath he had made with King Abimelech. Scientists today have discovered ancient wells in that region that have tamarisk trees growing around them.

Abraham Tested
Genesis 22:1 – 22:19

We have seen this story on television. We have heard it many times in Sunday School. It's a story of a man tested by God to sacrifice the one thing that was most important to him – his son Isaac. It's a story of obedience. But, let's see by reading the story for ourselves:

Isaac was God's promise to a 100 year old man who had been waiting a long time for it's arrival. Isaac was Abraham's son – a special gift from God. But, we already knew that.

The verses begin by stating that God tested Abraham. God calls out to him and tells him the plan. He wanted Abraham to take his son, Isaac, to a region in Moriah (which is about 50 miles away) and sacrifice him as a burnt offering on one of the mountains that He would show him. Did you catch that? Isaac was to be a burnt offering – as in fire and human flesh, like a steak cooked on a grill. Abraham had to do this to the one he loved for the One he loved most. This would have been hard to do.

Abraham didn't hesitate. He didn't sit around and think on it or negotiate with God about it. It says that, early the next morning, he saddled up his donkey and took two of his servants and his son. They took enough cut wood and headed to the place God had told him. It took them three days to get there. That took dedication. The first thing Abraham did was take his son to the place and worshiped. Then, he returned and gathered the stuff he needed. Abraham and Isaac went back and got things ready.

Isaac said (paraphrasing), "Hey, Dad? The fire and wood are here. Where's the sacrificial lamb? I think we forgot to bring it."

Abraham replied (paraphrasing), "Don't worry. God will provide it."

I wonder what would have happened if Abraham immediately told Isaac that he would be the sacrifice. Would Isaac have ran away? Would Isaac have fought back? Well, we know he wouldn't have called 9-1-1 because phones weren't invented yet.

As soon as they reach the place where the sacrifice would be made, Abraham builds the altar and arranges the wood. He then ties his son up and lays him on the altar. He grabs the knife to kill him. But, before he could follow through with it, an angel of the Lord yells down to him, "Abraham! Abraham! Do not lay a hand on the boy." God realized then that Abraham's heart was truly dedicated to Him. He let Isaac live. To finish the sacrifice, God provided Abraham with a ram instead. Abraham names this place The Lord Will Provide.

God blessed Abraham for what he had done by promising to make his descendants as numerous as the stars in the sky and sands on the seashore. He also tells him that his descendants would take possession of the cities of their enemies. Also, through his offspring all nations on Earth would be blessed. Abraham was truly rewarded for his act of obedience to God.

What can we learn? For one, if our parents invite us to go with them to make a burnt sacrifice to God, and they don't bring anything for a sacrifice, it would be best to stay home. But, on a serious note, obedience to God shows our love to Him and our faith in Him. God blesses those who are obedient to Him. The next time we feel like God is telling us to do something, it would be wise for us to do it. You agree?

Nahor's Sons
Genesis 22:20 – 22:24

In just four verses, we get a quick genealogy of Abraham's brother, Nahor. This is an addition to what we have already read in Genesis 11:10 – 11:32:

Nahor and his wife, Milcah
- Uz

- Buz
- Kemuel
- Kesed
- Hazo
- Pildash
- Jidlaph
- Bethuel

Nahor and his concubine, Reumah
- Tebah
- Gaham
- Tahash
- Maacah

The Death Of Sarah
Genesis 23:1 – 23:20

Sarah dies at Kiriath Arba (Hebron) in the land of Canaan at the ripe old age of 127 years old. At the funeral, Abraham speaks to the Hittites that were in attendance, "Sell me some property so that I can bury my wife." Keep in mind, Abraham was still an alien in the land and had no where to bury Sarah. It was just a man and his bride corpse and a group of mourners in attendance.

The Hittites, who highly respected Abraham, said, "Sir, you are a mighty prince among us. Bury her in whatever tomb you choose."

Abraham chose a cave that was owned by a man named Ephron. He wanted the Hittites to go and talk to him on his behalf, but as it turned out, Ephron was already in attendance. He heard everything that Abraham had said. Instead of selling the cave to Abraham, Ephron was willing to give it to him for free. Abraham didn't want the free handout, but was willing to pay the full price for it. The price? Four hundred shekels of silver. This is the equivalent of about $4500 today.

In today's market, that would have been a great deal. But, back in the day, it was considered high (possibly double the market value). Actually, the way Middle Eastern shopkeepers did business back then was to start their pricing high and let their customers negotiate with them. Maybe they could settle for a price that was much lower. Abraham accepted the first offer. And why didn't Abraham just accept the land as a free gift? Maybe Abraham knew that if he did, it would have offended Ephron. Ephron probably would have changed his mind about the whole deal and Abraham wouldn't have gotten anything. Another thing that interested me was that it wasn't a common practice for Hittites to sell their property to foreigners. I guess Abraham was an exception.

Abraham paid the price and was deeded the land, the cave and all of the trees that bordered the land. The place was in Machpelah near Mamre (which is in Hebron) in the land of Canaan.

Isaac and Rebekah
Genesis 24:1 – 24:67

Abraham was old and God had blessed him greatly. At this point in his life, he was focused on the future, especially on the future of his son, Isaac. He wanted him to marry someone special that would help him carry on the family name. He spoke to his chief servant; the one that was in charge of everything Abraham had.

"Promise me that you will not get my son a wife from the daughters of the Canaanites."

The agreement was made by the chief servant by putting his hand under Abraham's thigh. This is similar to how we make agreements when we shake hands or sign a document in the presence of a notary public, except their way was a little bit more weirder. It was almost like grabbing each other's butt. If you did something like that today, you would probably walk away with a black eye. But, that was then and this is now. Times do change.

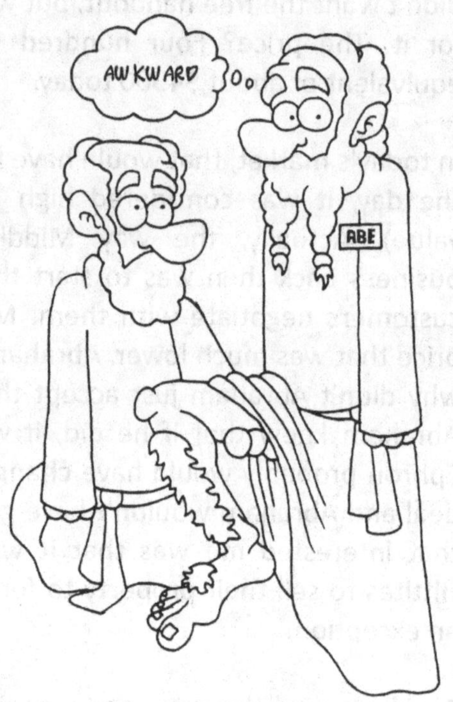

Even though Abraham was living in Canaan, he wanted his chief servant to go to the country where Abraham came from and select from his own people. This is where he wanted Isaac's future wife to come from. The chief servant agreed but he had a question.

"What if the woman won't come with me to Canaan to marry Isaac? You want me to take him to her?"

Abraham's answer was 'no'. Actually, his answer was more detailed.

"God will send an angel ahead of you and will select his wife in advance. All you got to do is go get her. If she will not come back to Canaan with you, our agreement will be void."

The chief servant takes ten of Abraham's camels with him on the journey and heads out for Aram Naharaim towards a place called Nahor. I can only assume that it takes ten camels to bring back one potential bride in Abraham's day. Maybe the women back then had a lot of luggage to carry. The chief servant parks the camels near a well outside of the town. It was evening time – a time when the women would come to draw water from the well. It was sorta like fishing. You go to where the fish are biting and you do it when its feeding time. The chief servant was pretty smart.

He prays to God for a successful catch and he was pretty specific on how he will know if the woman he sees is the right one for Isaac. He wanted her to be the one that offers him a drink from the well - not only for him, but also for his camels. Before he could finish praying, a woman walks up to the well. Her name was Rebekah. She was the daughter of Bethuel (son of Milcah – the wife of Abraham's brother Nahor). That's interesting. Rebekah was Isaac's first cousin.

"Please give me a little water from your jar." the chief servant asks.

Rebekah offers him water from her jar. When he finishes drinking, she goes over to the well and draws water for his camels. It was then that he knew that she was the one. He reaches for a gold nose ring and two gold bracelets that he brought for this special occasion. The nose ring weighed one beka (roughly 6 grams – today's market value is about $250) and the bracelets weighed ten shekels (roughly 100 grams – today's market value is about $4100). I guess the purpose of knowing this information in the Bible is to let the reader know how much money Abraham was investing in this engagement. It definitely wasn't something from a bubble gum machine.

And what about that gift of a nose ring? Was it cool for the ladies back then to wear nose rings? Was it the latest trend in fashion? From what I've read, it was simply how the women back in the day wore their wedding ring. In America, we wear ours on the 'ring' finger of our left hand. They wore theirs on their nose. If you think about it, it wasn't a bad idea. A person's face is usually the first thing you see when you meet them. The instant sight of a nose ring on a woman would let someone know that they were married. It makes perfect sense to me. I just don't think I could convince my wife to start wearing hers on her nose. But, I'll give it a try.

Rebekah was a beautiful virgin woman with a caring heart. I don't think the chief servant was concerned about her looks. Based on his prayer to God, he was looking for someone that was humble with a kind spirit. He felt that this kind of woman would make the perfect wife for Isaac.

In the next remaining verses, the chief servant learns who her parents were. He meets her brother, Laban. And he gets to spend the night in her family's house. He explains to everyone what his purpose was for being there and they accept him as being sent from God. They allow their daughter to go with him to marry his master, Isaac. There's a lot of conversation that went on between them. In addition to giving Rebekah the nose ring and bracelets, the chief servant also gave the family extravagant gifts. But, in the end, Rebekah leaves with him along with her nurse. Nurse?

I'm not really sure why a nurse was needed. Did Rebekah have some kind of medical condition that required the constant need for a nurse? I don't know. It's what the Bible says and I don't want to make assumptions. Maybe she was just an important person in Rebekah's life for the Bible to mention her. In Chapter 35, it tells us the nurse's name:

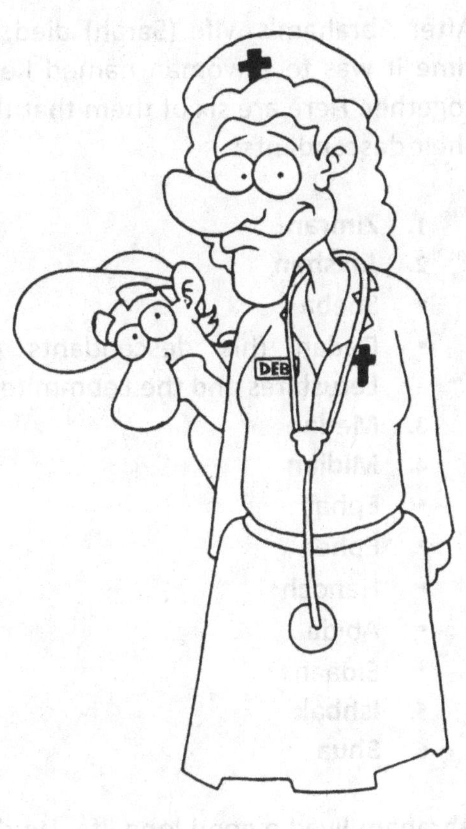

But Deborah Rebekah's nurse died, and she was buried beneath Bethel under an oak: and the name of it was called Allonbachuth. - Genesis 35: 8

Rebekah meets her future husband, Isaac, in Beer Lahai Roi in a field where he was meditating. She puts on a veil and covers herself as part of a customary bridal thing. It was love at first sight. So, Isaac invites her to come to his mother's tent and he marries her. Happily ever after? I'm not sure yet. We're only half way into the book of Genesis.

The Death Of Abraham
Genesis 25:1 – 25:11

After Abraham's wife (Sarah) died, he gets married again. This time it was to a woman named Keturah and they had children together. Here are six of them that the Bible mentions along with their descendants:

1. **Zimran**
2. **Jokshan**
   - Sheba
   - Dedan (his descendants were the Asshurites, the Letushites and the Leummites)
3. **Medan**
4. **Midian**
   - Ephah
   - Epher
   - Hanoch
   - Abida
   - Eldaah
5. **Ishbak**
6. **Shua**

Abraham lived a good long life. He died at 175 years old. He was buried in the same cave that his wife, Sarah, was buried in – in the field that he bought from the Hittities. Abraham left everything he owned to his son, Isaac. But, while he was living, he gave gifts to the sons of his concubines. He also sent these sons away from Isaac, to the land of the east. I guess he wanted to keep the sons separated because Isaac was his principle heir to his property.

After Abraham's death, God blessed Isaac, who was living near Beer Lahai Roi.

Ishmael's Sons
Genesis 25:12 – 25:18

Ishmael was Abraham's son that came from Sarah's maidservant, Hagar. From these verses, we discover a little bit about Ishmael and his descendants. Here are the names of his sons (and twelve tribal rulers according to their settlements and camps) in order of their birth:

1. **Nebaioth**
2. **Kedar**
3. **Adbeel**
4. **Mibsam**
5. **Mishma**
6. **Dumah**
7. **Massa**
8. **Hadad**
9. **Tema**
10. **Jetur**
11. **Naphish**
12. **Kedemah**

Ishmael died at 137 years old. His descendants settled in the area of Havilah to Shur near the border of Egypt. They all lived in hostility towards one another. That means they couldn't get along.

The Story Of Isaac

Jacob and Esau
Genesis 25:19 – 25:34

The verses begin with a little recap of who the main characters will be. Basically, there's two:

1. **Isaac** (son of Abraham)
2. **Rebekah** (daughter of Bethuel – the Aramean from Paddan Aram and sister of Laban – the Aramean)

Rebekah becomes pregnant with twins and it seems that she is having some complications. It's like the two babies inside her are wrestling with one another. She didn't know what was going on, so she asked the Lord about it. His reply:

And the LORD said unto her, Two nations are in thy womb, and two manner of people shall be separated from thy bowels; and the

99

one people shall be stronger than the other people; and the elder shall serve the younger. - Genesis 25: 23

Basically, there are two nations (tribal leaders) within her belly. Even though they are twins, they will be different from one another. One will be the strong one – the older one will serve the younger one. I guess now all we got to do is wait and see which baby comes out first.

Isaac was 60 years old when he became the proud father of a set of twins. He had prayed to God for a child, and just like Abraham (his father), he was getting up in age, so God finally blessed him. The first baby to arrive was a boy and he came out red. He was all covered in hair. They named him Esau. Can you imagine that? A red hairy baby boy. I imagine that wasn't a proud moment for Isaac. He may have been too embarrassed for anybody to see his new son.

This reminds me of when my son was born. He was a little stubborn at birth and didn't want to come out the natural way that most babies come out of the birth canal. The doctor had to use one of them vacuum suckers with the hoses attached. I guess there was so much suction going on that the process warped the shape of my son's head. He came out looking like E.T. from the Steven Spielberg movie from the 80's. He looked deformed. And when visitors stopped by to see my new son, I kept his head covered up with a hospital blanket. I didn't want them to see the horror. Fortunately for me, a few weeks later his head finally decided to reshape itself and he started looking like a normal baby. I could finally remove the blanket.

The next child born to Isaac and Rebekah came out with his hand grasping the heel of Esau. They named him Jacob. I'm sure there's some symbolism in why these babies arrived in the world the way the did; one all red and hairy and the other grabbing his brother's heel. There's definitely something there. Hopefully, we can get the answers from the Bible.

The boys grew up. Esau became a skilled hunter. He liked hanging out in the woods and doing activities that kept him outside. His brother, Jacob, was more of your quiet homely type. He liked spending time at home and would have been considered a 'homebody' or a 'recluse' in today's terminology. Their parents had their 'favorite' child. That's sad to admit, but the reality is that we all have that one child that we can relate to a little more than the other. Isaac was also the 'outdoors' type and loved Esau. Maybe he liked the idea of having a son that he could go fishing with. On the other hand, Rebekah's favorite son was Jacob. Maybe she was a 'homebody' too and now she could share this antisocial behavior with her son, Jacob. Together, they could do things around the home. In verse 29, it tells us that Jacob was cooking, so maybe that was something that he and his Mom did together.

Beginning in verse 29, there's something going on that is very important. Esau sells his birthright to his brother, Jacob, over a bowl of stew. That just sounds weird, so let's dig into this a little bit more:

Jacob was cooking some stew. Esau just came in from hunting and was starving. Here's the full conversation (paraphrased) between Esau and Jacob:

Esau: Hurry up! Give me some of that red stew. I'm starving!

Jacob: First sell me your birthright.

Esau: OK! Here! You can have it! Look! I'm about to die. I don't need my birthright anyway.

Jacob: Swear to me first.

Esau: OK. I swear. Now give me that stew!

So, Esau did. Jacob gave him some bread and lentil stew. Esau ate it and got up and left. The Bible ends with the statement that 'Esau despised his birthright'.

As I read all of this over and over trying to figure it all out, the only thing that comes to mind is that:

1. Esau made a drastic decision to solve a simple personal problem without thinking of his future.
2. Why didn't Jacob just give Esau the stew? He knew his brother was hungry. If you think about it, Esau was probably the one who provided the lentils for the soup anyway. Was Jacob being greedy? Or, was he simply fulfilling the prophecy that God gave his mother, Rebekah, before they were born?
3. What is a birthright anyway? From what I've read, a birthright was given to the first born son. It included a double portion of the family inheritance, plus the honor of one day becoming the family's leader. The oldest son had the choice of selling this birthright or giving it away. But if he does, he loses both the material goods and the leadership position. Esau didn't think about all of this, so he 'despised' his birthright by disregarding the spiritual blessings that would come from keeping it.

That's what I got from all of this.

Isaac and Abimelech
Genesis 26:1 – 26:35

There was a famine in the land and Isaac went to see Abimelech, the king of the Philistines in Gerar. I guess he was concerned about the economy and the food supply situation. He may of wanted to know what the king was going to do about it.

God appeared to Isaac and told him, "Do not go to Egypt. Live in the land where I tell you to live. Stay in this land for a while. I will be with you and will bless you." He also reminded him of the promised blessing that He had given to his father, Abraham. So, Isaac stayed in Gerar.

When Issac and Rebekah went to visit the king, they did the same thing that his father did back when he and Sarah traveled there. They told everyone in the city that they were brothers and sisters. Just like Abraham, Isaac feared that he would be killed and his wife taken away. It's like a repeat of Abraham's story. The strange thing to me about this scheme is that they entered the king's land with nothing and they left with some form of material gain — animals, money, etc. It's the same scenario, but with different characters. This time it was with Isaac and Rebekah.

Let's back up a little bit. Isaac and Rebekah were cousins and they were married. In the USA, this would be considered incest in many of our states. For the most part, it is frowned upon and considered 'icky'. Even though some of us are guilty of having 'childhood fun' with our cousins, like playing games such as Spin The Bottle and Truth Or Dare, we knew deep down not to take this game too far by marrying them. Cousins are just practicing tools to get us prepared for real-life relationships in the future. Everyone knows this. Right? Don't lie.

COUSINS PREPARE US FOR FUTURE RELATIONSHIPS.

Undoubtedly, back in the day, marrying cousins wasn't that big of a deal. It was all about maintaining the family bloodline. They were still many years away from receiving the marriage and relationship laws from Moses. Even though later those laws forbid them to have relations with people 'that were kin', the term 'cousins' were never mentioned in this law. So, I guess this was OK.

After being in the city for a while, the king noticed from his window that Isaac was caressing his wife, Rebekah, in what would appear to be in an inappropriate way. It was just something that brothers and sisters didn't do, so King Abimelech questioned Isaac about it. Isaac tells him the truth and the king pardons him. In fact, the king offers him and his family protection from the weirdos living in the land and they are allowed to live there.

God blessed Isaac. He planted crops that produced a hundredfold in the same year. He became excessively wealthy and his wealth kept on growing. He had so many flocks, herds and servants. The Philistines were jealous. It got so out of control that Abimelech had to confront him about it:

"Isaac, you've got to go. Sorry, man. You need to move. You have become to powerful for us."

So, Isaac moved away and settled in the Valley of Gerar. His first personal mission was to reopen a bunch of the wells that had been dug during the time of his father, Abraham. He even gave the wells the same name his father had given them. You see, after Abraham died, the Philistines covered all of these wells up so that they couldn't be used. Isaac was basically revisiting the work that his father had started. This didn't come without opposition.

It seemed that wherever Isaac dug a well, someone immediately took ownership of it. Two of them are mentioned:

- **Esek**
- **Sitnah**

However, there was one well that he dug that no one argued with him about. He named it Rehoboth. It was a sign to him that the Lord was giving him the 'room' he needed to branch out so that he would flourish in the land.

After digging wells, he went on up to Beersheba. The Lord appeared to him that night and gave him encouragement. He also reminded him of the blessings he would receive because of the faithfulness of his father, Abraham. Isaac built an altar to God. He also pitched a tent and his servants dug another well. While they were in Beersheba, King Abimelech came down to visit him all the way from Gerar. He brought along his personal advisor (Ahuzzah) and the commander of his military (Phicol). Isaac was shocked of their visit.

"Why are ya'll here?" Isaac asked. Their last encounter was a little heated when the king told him to get off his property a few verses back. Remember?

They tell Isaac, "We saw clearly that the Lord was with you. There needs to be a sworn agreement between us – you and us. Let's make a treaty with you that you will do us no harm."

Issac prepared a feast for the gentlemen and they ate and drank. Early the next morning, they swore an oath to each other. When they finished, Isaac sent them on their way and the men left him in peace. It was a done deal.

That same day, Isaac's servant came to him with some great news. They got water from one of the wells that they dug. Isaac named it Shibah.

The last two verses talks a little bit about Esau (Isaac's red hairy son – remember him?). From here, we learn that Esau got married at the age of 40 to two women:

- **Judith** (daughter of Beeri the Hittite)
- **Basemath** (daughter of Elon the Hittite)

Esau and his marital arrangement caused a lot of grief to his parents - Isaac and Rebekah. It could have been because Esau married pagan women. Can you imagine how their children would turn out? I also can't help but think back to when Abraham was choosing a wife for Isaac. He specifically said that he didn't want one from the land of Canaan. And now we see that Esau made his choices from there and he didn't even allow his father to choose for him. I can see why there was grief in the family.

Jacob Gets Isaac's Blessing
Genesis 27:1 – 27:40

Isaac was getting old and blind. He knew that he was going to die, but just didn't know when. He wanted to go ahead make the proper arrangements before his death. He calls for his firstborn son, Esau. He wanted to give him his blessing.

Isaac tells Esau to go hunting and to prepare him some food. Since they were very close, Esau knew what foods his father liked to eat. So, he heads out to the open fields and does what he does best – hunt.

Rebekah overheard the conversation that Isaac had with Esau. She knew that he was about to bless him. But, since Jacob was her favorite son, she tells Jacob to gather food for her to prepare, but to do it before Esau returns. She knew her husband was getting blind, and thought if Jacob gave him food first, Issac would think that he was Esau. He would then unknowingly bless Jacob instead. This would be considered trickery and a lie. Jacob had doubts about the plan that his mother had come up with. He didn't think it would work. Actually, if his father had discovered the truth, he would have cursed him. It would turn out to be a bad thing for him in the end.

I like the point that Jacob made about him and his brother that would separate them in the eyes of their father. It was their skin type. Esau was hairy and Jacob had smooth skin. If their father touched Jacob, he would automatically know it was him. But, his mother was persistent about the plan. If Isaac found out, she would take the fall. So, they put her plan in motion.

Jacob gathered the food and gave it to his mother. She put her skills to work in the kitchen and made something delicious. She also took some of Esau's finest clothes and put them on Jacob. To make the plan succeed, she covered Jacob's hands and the smooth part of his neck with goatskin. She was determined to fool her husband and sent her son to him with the food that she prepared. Here's how it went down (paraphrased):

Jacob: Father?
Isaac: Yes, my son. Who is it?
Jacob: I am Esau – your firstborn son. I have done everything you told me. Sit up. Eat some of this food so that you can give me your blessing.
Isaac: Hmm... how did you prepare it so quickly?
Jacob: The Lord made it all possible.
Isaac: Come here so that I can touch you. I want to make sure that you are Esau.

<Jacob stepped closer to his father. Isaac touched him>

Isaac: Hmm... the voice is the voice of Jacob, but the hands are the hands of Esau. Are you really Esau?
Jacob: Yep. It is I – all hairy and junk.
Isaac: Bring me some of your food so that I can give you my blessing.

<Jacob brings him the food. Isaac eats it and drinks the wine that he brought>

Isaac: Come closer, my son, so that I can kiss you.

<Jacob comes closer. Isaac kisses him. When he gets a whiff of Esau's clothes, he then blesses him>

See, the smell of my son is as the smell of a field which the LORD hath blessed: Therefore God give thee of the dew of heaven, and the fatness of the earth, and plenty of corn and wine: Let people serve thee, and nations bow down to thee: be lord over thy brethren, and let thy mother's sons bow down to thee: cursed be every one that curseth thee, and blessed be he that blesseth thee. - Genesis 27: 27-29

After Isaac blesses him, Jacob leaves the scene. Next thing you know, the real Esau walks in with the food that he prepared for him. Now, it's fixing to get all weird up in here.

Esau: Father, sit up. Eat some of the food that I have prepared for you so that you can give me my blessing.
Isaac: Who are you?
Esau: It's me – your firstborn son, Esau.
Isaac (trembling): Who was that person that came before you and brought me food? Whoever it was, I blessed him instead.
Esau (bursting out in a loud and bitter cry): Bless me! Bless me too, father!
Isaac: Sorry, but your brother deceitfully came and stole your blessing.
Esau: Jacob? That joker has deceived me twice. He took my birthright and now he has taken my blessing. Father, do you have any more of those blessings lying around that you can give me?
Isaac: Nope. I'm all out. Hey. Just so you know. I made Jacob lord over you and all of y'all's relatives will now be his servants. I have sustained him with grain and new wine. So, what could I possibly offer you, my son?
Esau: So, you're telling me that you only have one blessing? Come on! You got to have an extra one lying around somewhere. Bless me, my father!

<Esau begins crying out loud>

Isaac's only answer to his son, Esau, was:

Behold, thy dwelling shall be the fatness of the earth, and of the dew of heaven from above; And by thy sword shalt thou live, and shalt serve thy brother; and it shall come to pass when thou shalt have the dominion, that thou shalt break his yoke from off thy neck. - Genesis 27: 39,40

Sounds like Esau will be living life on Earth as a poor man. He will live by the sword and will serve his brother, Jacob. And when he gets tired of carrying all of these hurtful feelings around, he will more than likely try and seek revenge. But, let's see how the story unfolds.

Jacob Flees To Laban
Genesis 27:41 – 28:9

Esau held a grudge against his brother, Jacob. This guy robbed him of his birthright and now his father's blessing. Esau felt betrayed and now he was pretty ticked off about it.

A 'blessing' and a 'birthright' was a serious thing back in ancient times. Also, a 'person's word' was binding (like a written contract is today), especially when it was a formal oath.

When Isaac was on his death bed, he performed a ceremony of blessing. This blessing was also when he officially handed over the birthright to the rightful heir. Even though the firstborn was entitled to the birthright, it wasn't actually his until the blessing was given. Before the blessing was given, the father could take the birthright from the oldest son and give it to a more deserving son. But, after the blessing was given, the birthright could no longer be taken away. It was 'sealed in stone' by the father's word. You with me? This is why most fathers back in the day waited until late in life to pronounce the blessing. This gave them time to determine which son truly deserved the birthright. Although Jacob had been given the birthright by his older brother many years before, he still needed his father's blessing to make it binding.

Esau knew he had been tricked. He was very angry about it. He didn't want to take action against his brother until his father died. Undoubtedly, Esau didn't realize he was talking out loud about his plans to kill Jacob because his mother, Rebekah, was told every word from unknown sources who were probably standing nearby listening to him. She quickly relayed the message to her younger son and gave him directions on what to do next. She told him to leave and stay at her brother's house. This was Labran and he lived in Haran. She had hoped that Esau would forget about what had happened to him and let his anger subside. After letting him cool down for a bit, she would then send for Jacob to return back home. She just didn't want two deaths in her family to happen on the same day. That would have been hard to bare.

The scene changes in verse 46. Rebekah is talking to her dying husband about the kind of women that lived in Canaan. They were Hittite women and she despised them. It could have had something to do with the Canaanite belief system – they were pagans. She didn't like any of it. She told Isaac that she didn't want their son, Jacob, marrying any of them. So, just like Abraham did with Isaac when he was younger, Isaac has a talk with Jacob. He gives him strict instructions to not marry a woman from Canaan. Instead, go to the land of Paddan Aram where his mother's father, Bethuel, lived. Take a wife from among the daughters of Laban (his mother's brother). Yes, he was to marry one of his cousins. It's starting to sound like a family tradition of marrying cousins. But hey, it's in the Bible.

When Esau heard about his father blessing Jacob and forbidding him to marry a Canaanite by sending him to Paddan Aram to find a wife, he decided to get married, too. Maybe he was trying to please his parents. Who knows? Esau went to Ishmael (Isaac's half-brother) and married Mahalath (Ishmael's daughter). Keep in mind, Esau already had two foreign wives (Genesis 26: 34). This would be his new addition (and she would be his step-cousin). Interesting.

The Story Of Jacob

Jacob Starts A Family
Genesis 28:10 – 28:22

Jacob traveled on from Beersheba to Haran. At sunset, he stopped for the night and camped out. Hotels weren't invented yet, so he camped outside on the ground. Actually, he used a stone for a pillow. It probably wasn't the best idea because a stone just wouldn't offer the same comfort for a good night's sleep as a fluffy pillow made from feathers. But, he did it anyway.

As he slept, he had a dream. He saw a stairway that began on Earth and went straight up to Heaven. Angels were going up and down the stairs and God was at the top. Jacob heard God make the promise that He had made to his ancestors many years back:

"I am the God of your father Abraham and Isaac. I will give you and your descendants the land that you are sleeping on. You will have so many descendants that it will be like counting dust in all directions – north, south, east and west. Everybody on Earth will be blessed through you and your offspring. I will be with you and will be watching over you wherever you go. One day I will bring you back to this land. I will not leave you until I have done what I have promised."

When Jacob woke up, he knew that he was in the presence of the Lord and this place that he was at was the gate of Heaven. He knew he had an encounter with God. I bet he was shaken a little. The next morning, he took the stone he used as a pillow and

made a pillar. That sounded funny, didn't it? In the South, that's what we call that fluffy thing in bed that we place our head on at night – pronounced *pil-ler.* Anyway, Jacob poured oil on it. This would be similar to creating a stone marker, so that if he crossed this path again, the stone would stand out for him to remember. The oil he used could have been olive oil and pouring it on the stone could have been his way of dedicating it. Or, he simply wanted to make the stone greasy so that it would be easier to see, but I seriously doubt it. It says in the next few verses that Jacob makes a vow, that the stone he set up as a pillar, will be God's house.

He named the place Bethel (even though it had already been named Luz). Bethel was about 10 miles north of Jerusalem and

60 miles north of Beersheba. It was also where Abraham made one of his first sacrifices when he entered the land. At first, Bethel became an important worship center. Later, it became a center for idol worship. That's interesting to know.

After Jacob pronounced the place's new name, he made a financial vow. In return of God's protection on this journey, plus any clothes and food that God provided him, Jacob vowed to give God back a tenth. This would be the first mention of a tithe. This would be very significant for the future generations to come.

Jacob Arrives In Paddan Aram
Genesis 29:1 – 29:14a

Jacob makes it to Paddam Aram. He meets a handful of shepherds who are gathering their sheep at a well. Basically, this spot is where the sheep get water. The process for doing this is by rolling a stone off the top off the well, getting the sheep water and then covering the well back up. No big deal, right?

After talking to the shepherds, he realizes that they know his uncle, Laban. He probably felt relieved because he had made it to his destination. As he stayed at the well a little longer, he meets his cousin, Rachel, who is also getting water for her sheep. Out of courtesy, Jacob does all the work for her and proceeds to give his cousin a kiss and then starts crying. Maybe he missed seeing his mother's side of the family. Maybe it had been years since they had seen each other. Maybe he felt guilty for 'swapping slobber' with a close relative. Who knows? Rachel got all excited about it too and runs off to tell her father. Let's just hope she tells him good news.

Laban hears the news and hurries to the well to meet Jacob. They hug and kiss (like all uncles and nephews did back then) and head back to Laban's house to further this family get together. I'm sure this was a happy time for their family and not something strange. Getting kisses from uncles isn't something we, as men, practice these days. Hugs and handshakes are about as far as we go with all of that. But, maybe back then, it was the thing to do.

Jacob Marries Leah And Rachel
Genesis 29:14b – 29:30

Jacob stays at his Uncle Laban's house for a whole month. I wouldn't consider him a moocher because he helped around the house doing the chores. It was probably his way of covering the costs of him staying there so long. I think that was a noble thing to do. I know, personally, I have had teenagers living in my house for years that didn't like picking up after themselves. I would have been grateful for the extra help. You know what I'm saying? It would have definitely made 'wanting them to stay' much easier for me.

Jacob's uncle was feeling a little bit guilty about him doing all of this work for him and offered to pay him instead. He asked him what would he charge for all his labor that he was providing.

Jacob didn't come up with an hourly rate nor a per job fee. Instead, he said he wanted to marry one of his daughters.

Laban had two daughters. Leah was the oldest and all we know about her was that she had weak eyes. I can only imagine that maybe she squinted a lot or bumped into stuff too much. Glasses or Lasik surgery weren't invented yet, so she probably struggled with her bad vision. Rachel was Laban's youngest daughter. The scriptures tells us that she had curves and was very beautiful. This was the daughter that Jacob liked the most. I think it was love at first sight back when they met at the well a few verses back.

Jacob worked a deal with his uncle. He offered to work for him for seven years in exchange for her hand in marriage. Laban agreed and Jacob worked for the seven year term of the agreement. At the end of the deal, Jacob came to collect.

"OK. My side of the agreement is complete. Where's my wife?"

Laban threw a party and invited a bunch of guests. They celebrated this new union. When it came time for the honeymoon, Laban delivered his oldest daughter (Leah) instead. I guess the room was dark and Jacob couldn't see. He woke up the next morning and realized he just had relations with the wrong girl. It wasn't with Rachel like he had hoped. It was with Leah — the weak-eyed sister. He was angry and wanted to know why Laban deceived him.

I guess Laban forgot to mention the 'marriage rule' before their agreement. It seems that it was their custom back in the day that the youngest daughter could not marry before the oldest. Maybe Laban used this rule as a way to finally get his daughter, Leah, hitched. Weak-eyed girls may not have been a man's first choice of a future wife. However, for a small 'work for me for another seven years', he could give his daughter Rachel to him to marry. So, he did. Jacob worked another seven years and finally receives Rachel as his wife.

Now, Jacob had two wives. However, he loved Rachel more than her sister, Leah. But, he kept them both anyway. Also, as an added bonus and parting gift, each of the wives came with their own personal maidservant (Zilpah and Bilhah). That's one man and four women living in his household. This can't be a good combination.

Jacob's Children
Genesis 29:31 – 30:24

There's a lot of relations going on in these verses. Actually, it's kind of confusing unless you read it slow and write it down.

It tells us that Rachel could not have children. However, we learn that Leah is so fertile that she keeps popping out babies left and right. Rachel gets desperate and makes her maidservant, Bilhah, have kids for her. Then, Leah stops having kids for a brief moment and makes her maidservant, Zilpah, have them for her, too. And then later, the two sisters are able to have kids once again and produce more. Here's what the 'baby outcome' looked like for poor Jacob:

With Rachel
- Joseph
- Benjamin (Genesis 35:18)

With Leah
- Reuban
- Simeon
- Levi
- Judah
- Issachar
- Zebulun
- Dinah

With Bilhah
- Dan
- Naphtali

With Zilpah
- Gad
- Asher

That's a grand total of thirteen kids! Jacob loved Rachel (who couldn't have kids) but was blessed with two. Leah never felt loved by Jacob and ended up with seven. The two maidservants were used by Leah and Rachel and produced four. Looks like a very messed up situation and a lot of mouths to feed to me. But, we will soon find out.

Jacob's Flock Increases
Genesis 30:25 – 30:43

After Rachel gave birth to Joseph, Jacob was ready to go back home. He had worked for his uncle, Laban, for a total of about twenty years. During this time, he had married two wives, which were Laban's daughters, and had a bunch of kids. He told his uncle it was time for them to go.

Laban sounded like he didn't want them to leave. He must have looked around at all of the great things that had happened around him because of Jacob being there and felt blessed. Maybe it was the joy of having all of his grandkids around him. It would be sad for him to see them all go. But, the scripture mentions that his livestock and flocks increased, which back then were considered the same as monetary gain. Laban had become very wealthy because of Jacob. Now it was time to put it to an end. Laban felt like he owed something to his nephew for all of his hard work.

"What do I owe you?" Laban asked Jacob.

Hopefully, Laban didn't have any extra daughters. Jacob already married two and didn't need any more.

"You don't owe me anything." Jacob replied. "But if you would do this one thing for me."

I imagine Laban put his wallet back into his pocket and now had this look of confusion on his face.

All Jacob wanted was all of Laban's speckled or spotted sheep, very dark colored lamb and every spotted or speckled goat. This would be his wages in return for all of the hard work he had done for his uncle. At this point, Laban probably thought his nephew was one nugget short of a Happy Meal. Who asks for crazy stuff like this? I have never seen a speckled sheep before and it wouldn't be my first choice of payment. But, he agreed to those terms and allowed Jacob to remove the weird looking animals from his herd.

After Jacob had done all of this, he does something kind of strange. He takes fresh-cut branches from poplar, almond and planes trees. He peels back the bark on them so that it leaves white stripes. He puts them in the watering troughs of the animals so that they could see them as they walked up and took a drink. When the thirsty animals came to the trough, and were in heat, they would mate in front of the branches. I don't understand this process or how it all works, but it somehow created a bunch of animals for Jacob. He, then, separated the weak animals from the strong ones and gave the weaker ones to his uncle. By doing so, Jacob became very rich.

What is going on?

Jacob told his uncle earlier, when he was getting some of his sheep, goat and lamb, that he would only take the spotted and speckled ones. Jacob also mentioned that, if anything other than that was found in his herd, it would be considered stolen. And Jacob didn't want to be known as a thief. It sounds like Jacob knew a way to create speckled and spotted animals through the use of certain tree branches and the chemicals they produced in water. This would be a 'science' thing (called animal biotechnology), which is kind of cool. You heard it here first, folks!

Jacob Flees From Laban
Genesis 31:1 – 31:21

Jacob heard a rumor that Laban's sons were telling everyone that he was a thief – a title that Jacob did not want. He actually did everything he could to prevent it. They said that the reason for Jacob's great wealth was because he stole everything from their father, Laban. Laban was beginning to feel this way, too. His attitude toward Jacob wasn't the way it used to be.

The Lord told Jacob to pack up his stuff and move back to the land of his fathers and relatives, but not to worry. He would be with him. I guess He felt that Jacob would worry because of the feelings his uncle and cousins had towards him. I mean, he had been with them for twenty years and had built a trusting relationship. If he left, he would appear that he was guilty of what they were accusing him of. That makes sense. Otherwise, moving back home to be with people that he knew doesn't seem to be something he should be worrying about.

Jacob gave word to Rachel and Leah to pack their stuff and get ready to move. He reminded them of how Laban had wronged him. He also told them of how it wasn't his fault that God blessed him and not Laban. Rachel and Leah were in agreement with him. They also felt like their father had wronged them, too. This made it easy for them to move without any regrets. So they loaded up the camels and headed to Canaan to be with Jacob's father, Isaac.

Laban Pursues Jacob
Genesis 31:22 – 31:55

Jacob and his wives had already been gone for three days when Laban found out that they were missing. So, he and his relatives loaded up their traveling gear and went looking for them. They traveled for seven days and met up with them in the hillside country of Gilead. That night, Laban had a dream where God told him, "Be careful not to say anything good or bad to Jacob." This was a warning from God to Laban to start no trouble.

In Gilead, Laban had camped where Jacob was. He confronted him by saying, "What have you done?" Laban had felt deceived. Jacob and his wives and the whole gang had left Laban's home without saying a word. I assume Laban woke up one morning and wondered, "Where did everybody go?"

Let's have a little sympathy for Laban for a moment. This guy felt like he was blessed and on top of the world. Jacob had lived with him for twenty years. And because of him, his livestock was growing and he was very wealthy. Life was good. Laban gets a husband for, not only 1 daughter, but 2 and they blessed him with a bunch of grandkids. This guy is living it up because all of this is happening right before his eyes and on his land. Jacob was getting wealthy too from the stuff

that Laban was giving him in the form of wages. God blessed these things and it made Laban's sons very jealous. They felt that Jacob was robbing their father. This is when Jacob decided to move. The sad thing about this move was that the things Laban considered blessings were being taken from him, too. He felt like he was being robbed. The reality was that the things he was holding on to were no longer his.

But, the fact remains that Laban was a self-centered person. He was always looking out for himself. You could see it in the way he treated others. A perfect example would be in how he made Jacob work for him for so long and using his daughters as bargaining chips. Are you seeing this, too?

In the remaining verses, Laban and Jacob made a covenant by piling up stones into a heap. Jacob agreed to never mistreat Laban's daughters and to never marry anyone else. They both agreed to deal with each other peacefully and never cross this heap where they made the covenant. Laban called this Jegar Sahadutha. Jacob named it Galeed (also called Mizpah). God was their witness as they settled their differences.

The next morning, Laban kisses his daughters and grandchildren and blesses them. He leaves and returns home.

Jacob Prepares To Meet Esau
Genesis 32:1 – 32:21

Jacob was getting ready to move on when he saw angels of God before him. He was amazed because he considered the place the camp of God. He even named it. He called it Mahanaim.

Jacob made plans to meet with his brother (Esau) that he hadn't seen in 20 years. He knew it wouldn't be a pleasant meeting, so he sent messengers ahead of him to the land of Seir; the country of Edom. This would give his brother a 'heads up' that he was coming and hoped his messengers would return with something good to say. Instead, they tell Jacob that his brother is heading their way with four hundred men. This didn't sound too good. It sounded more like a warning of an upcoming battle. Keep in mind, Esau made a vow to kill him a few chapters back (Genesis 27:41).

In fear, Jacob divides his people and animals into two groups. That way, if his brother attacked one of them, the other group could possibly escape. Jacob immediately began to pray and reminded God of His promises made to him. Jacob was worried.

Jacob camped out and spend the night there in Mahanaim. He started looking around at the things he had and selected a gift that he could give his brother. Instead of a gift card at your local home improvement store, he rounded up 200 female goats, 20 male goats, 200 ewes, 20 rams, 30 female camels with their young, 40 cows, 10 bulls, 20 female donkeys and 10 male donkeys. He instructed his servants to go ahead of him and give these gifts to his brother and let him know where they came from. Also, let him know that he would be traveling not too far behind them.

Jacob's 'gift plan' was a hopeful way of easing the anger that Esau had against him. By sending his servants ahead of time with these gifts, Jacob hoped that Esau wouldn't be so angry by the time they met each other face to face. As the servants traveled onward, Jacob stayed behind and spent the night in the camp.

128

These were probably great gifts for someone that made a living raising livestock. This was just as good as money. For someone like me, receiving a gift like this would have been more like a curse. What would I do with that many animals? And who's gonna clean up all this poop? Just give me the gift card to a home improvement store.

Jacob Wrestles With God
Genesis 32:22 – 32:32

That night, Jacob got up and took his wives, maidservants and 11 sons across the ford of the Jabbok. After they had made it safely across, he also sends over all of his possessions. Jacob was alone there in Mahanaim.

It tells us in verse 24 that a man wrestled with him all night. This man, after discovering that he couldn't overpower him, decides to touch the socket of Jacob's hip (maybe a pull or a twist) causing him to be inflicted with pain. All of a sudden, the man says, "Let me go. The sun's up." OK. Who is this man? Why were they fighting? And who calls off a fight just because the

sun rises in the sky? Was this a vampire? I seriously doubt it. Even though I don't have all of the answers to these questions, I did find something interesting about it:

To best answer this question, it helps to know, among other things, that deep-seated family hostilities characterized Jacob's life. He was a determined man; some would consider him to be ruthless. He was a con artist, a liar, and a manipulator. In fact, the name Jacob not only means 'deceiver', but more literally it means 'grabber'.

To know Jacob's story is to know his life was one of never-ending struggles. Though God promised Jacob that, through him, would come not only a great nation, but a whole company of nations. He was a man full of fears and anxieties. We now come to a pivotal point in his life when he is about to meet his brother (Esau), who has vowed to kill him. All Jacob's struggles and fears are about to be realized. Sick of his father-in-law's treatment, Jacob has fled Laban, only to encounter his embittered brother, Esau. Anxious for his very life, Jacob concocted a bribe and sent a caravan of gifts along with his women and children across the River Jabbok in hopes of pacifying his brother. Now physically exhausted, alone in the desert wilderness, facing sure death, he's divested of all his worldly possessions. In fact, he's powerless to control his fate. He collapses into a deep sleep on the banks of the Jabbok River. With his father-in-law behind him and Esau before him, he was too spent to struggle any longer.

But only then did his real struggle begin. Fleeing his family history had been bad enough; wrestling with God Himself was a different matter altogether. That night an angelic stranger visited Jacob. They wrestled throughout the night until daybreak, at which point the stranger crippled Jacob with a blow to his hip that disabled him with a limp for the rest of his life. It was by then Jacob knew what had happened: "I saw God face to face, and yet my life was spared" (Genesis 32:30). In the process, Jacob (the deceiver) received a new name, Israel, which likely means 'He struggles with God'. However, what is most important occurs at the conclusion of that struggle. We read that God 'blessed him there'(Genesis 32:29).

In Western culture and even in our churches, we celebrate wealth and power, strength, confidence, prestige, and victory. We despise and fear weakness, failure, and doubt. Though we know that a measure of vulnerability, fear, discouragement and depression come with normal lives, we tend to view these as signs of failure or even a lack of faith. However, we also know that in real life, naive optimism and the glowing accolades of glamour and success are a recipe for discontent and despair. Sooner or later, the cold, hard realism of life catches up with most of us. The story of Jacob pulls us back to reality.

The apostle Paul experienced similar discouragements and fears: "We were harassed at every turn—conflicts on the outside, fears within" (2 Corinthians 7: 5). But, in truth, God does not want to leave us with our trials, our fears, our battles in life. What we come to learn in our conflicts of life is that God proffers us a corresponding divine gift. It is through Him that we can receive the power of conversion and transformation, the gift of not only surrender, but freedom, and the gifts of endurance, faith and courage.

In the end, Jacob does what we all must do. He confronts his failures, his weaknesses, his sins, all the things that are hurting him... and faces God. Jacob wrestled with God all night. It was an exhausting struggle that left him crippled. It was only after he came to grips with God and ceased his struggling, realizing that he could not go on without Him, that he received God's blessing (Genesis 32:29).

What we learn from this remarkable incident in the life of Jacob is that our lives are never meant to be easy. This is especially true when we take it upon ourselves to wrestle with God and His will for our lives. We also learn that as Christians, despite our trials and tribulations, our strivings in this life are never devoid of God's presence, and His blessing inevitably follows the struggle, which can sometimes be messy and chaotic. Real growth experiences always involve struggle and pain.

Jacob's wrestling with God at the Jabbok that dark night reminds us of this truth: though we may fight God and His will for us, in truth, God is so very good. As believers in Christ, we may well struggle with Him through the loneliness of night, but by daybreak His blessing will come.

Wow! I couldn't have said it better myself.

Jacob Meets Esau
Genesis 33:1 – 33:20

Jacob looked up and saw in the distance that his brother Esau was coming to see him. He even brought along 400 men. This was probably a scary sight. A battle was about to brew.

He divided up his family. The way I read it sounded it like he put his family on the front line in order of their importance to him or by who he loved the most. The maidservants and their children were placed up front. Behind them, he placed Leah and her children. And in the back row, he placed Rachel and their son, Joseph. That's what it sounded like to me. But, either way, Jacob heads past the front line and bows down to the ground seven times as he gets closer to his brother. Jacob was treating him like royalty or he was presenting an act of surrender and request for mercy. I'm not really sure.

A surprising thing happened. Esau ran towards Jacob and gave him a hug. They kissed like brothers do and started crying. All of their anger and worries were gone. It was like nothing had ever happened. I guess time can mend all wounds.

I believe Esau's original plan was to wipe Jacob out. Why else would he have brought 400 men? But something happened. His heart was changed. It turned out to be a good reunion between two brothers. Jacob introduced him to his wives and children. I'm sure it was a like a family get together. A lot had happened in twenty years and they probably had lots of things to catch up on. After talking for a while, Esau heads back to Seir. Even though Jacob tells him that he would be heading there too, he decides to go to Succoth instead. It was here that he built a place for himself and shelter for his animals.

It also mentions that Jacob bought a plot of land from the sons of Hamor (the father of Shechem) for a hundred pieces of silver. This was in the land of Canaan. On this property, he builds an altar and calls it 'El Elohe Israel'. I learned that this means "God is the God of Israel'.

Dinah and the Shechemites

Genesis 34:1 – 34:31

Jacob and Leah had a daughter named Dinah. She was up in age and went out to visit the women of the land. I guess there was a cool hangout spot for the ladies somewhere in town and Dinah wanted to hang out with them. The ruler of that area (Shechem – son of Hamor the Hivite) saw her. It was love at first sight and he acted upon his feelings and violated her. To me, it sounded like he raped her. But, it says that he loved her and that he asked his father

(Hamor) to get this girl as his wife. I'm not really sure what's going on here, but whatever happened, it made Dinah's family very angry.

Hamor visits with Jacob and his sons and asked for them to allow Dinah to marry his son. Actually, he wanted Jacob's family to intermarry with his. It would become one big happy family with benefits. Jacob could live wherever he wanted to, start a business there and own as much property as he could afford. Sounded like a pretty good deal.

Shechem also talked with Jacob and Dinah's brothers. He wanted their favor and offered to pay whatever price they asked for his daughter. And whatever gift Jacob wanted, he would provide no matter what the cost. All Shechem wanted was for Dinah to be his wife.

Dinah's brothers weren't too happy about this rapist asking to marry their sister. Shechem was royalty, so they couldn't gang up on him and beat the crap out of him. They would have been arrested or worse. So, how do you get this creep to change his mind? Well, they gave him an obstacle that he probably couldn't climb over. They said, that because of their beliefs, he would have to be circumcised including all of the males in his land. That was the only way he could marry their sister. Also, by doing so, they would agree to intermarry with them and become one people. The brothers were hoping this would be an impossibility, so they could take their sister and be done.

Hamor and his son, Shechem, saw no problem with this proposal. Shechem didn't waste any time about it and got the ball rolling with the menfolk in his town. Everybody got circumcised. Three days later, while the men were still in pain, Jacob's two sons (Simeon and Levi) took their swords and headed to the town that Shechem lived. They killed every male. After killing Shechem, they took Dinah back home. They also looted the town. They took all of their animals, their wealth and even their women and children.

Jacob wasn't too happy with how this was handled. Their actions would create problems for him with the Canaanites and the Perizzites. He was worried that they would join forces one day and seek revenge by destroying his household.

Simeon and Levi felt like they did the right thing. In their mind, they restored honor to their sister. For the time being, they also prevented intermarriage between the two families.

Jacob Returns To Bethel
Genesis 35:1 – 35:15

God tells Jacob to go to Bethel and live. While he was there, build an altar to Him. So, Jacob gathered up his household. But first, he told them to get rid of their foreign gods that they had, purify themselves and to change their clothes. Why would these people, who worshiped God, have foreign idols in their possession? And were these idols portable? What were they anyway?

This could be things like a Buddha statue. It could also be talking about things such as lucky charms. This could be stuff such as a lucky rabbits foot or maybe a lucky coin. Maybe somebody kept a four leaf clover in a picture frame or had a horseshoe hanging on their wall at home. These are all things that some of us have that we really don't think much about, but some people do. I believe idols are anything that we put before God. Jacob believed that idols shouldn't have a place in the home at all. He was concerned about his people's spiritual focus.

The people gave Jacob their idols and their ear rings. He buried them under the oak at Shechem. Ear rings? Are ear rings a bad thing? Jewelry wasn't a sin. Was it? From what I've read, ear rings worn in Jacob's day were many times worn by people as a good luck charm to ward off evil. It was a pagan thing. Jacob buried all of the pagan-related items so that it would not influence his people or remind them of foreign gods. He wanted a clean slate.

As Jacob and his people set out, there was a 'terror of God' upon all of the towns around them and nobody pursued them. Don't forget. Two of Jacob's sons are now fugitives and wanted for mass murder. They murdered a whole town of men. And now they were able to travel without anyone trying to arrest them or even kill them.

They made it to Bethel (aka Luz) in the land of Canaan. Jacob built the altar, just as God requested, and gave it a name: El Bethel. It sorta has a Spanish ring to it, but I'm sure it's not. Special places get named in the Bible, especially when God has something to do with the area or by His presence being there. These names have meanings. El Bethel would mean 'the place where God revealed Himself' while Jacob was fleeing from his brother'. The name is now just as important as the place. This information would be handed down for many generations to come as a reminder of what God had done. Names like that are all in Genesis and the Old Testament.

This could apply to us in our lives, too. Are there special places where you remember feeling the presence of God? Or how about places where you received the answer to your prayers? Those places have become memorable to you. You may not have named it, but it will definitely be a place you will never forget.

Deborah. Remember her? This was Rebekah's nurse that we read about a few chapters back. Well, she died. She was buried under an oak tree below Bethel. It got named, too. Allon Bacuth was the name given and it means 'oak of weeping'. This wasn't the only thing that got named. Jacob gets renamed by God. He named him Israel. In Hebrew, that name Israel means 'may God prevail'.

The Deaths Of Rachel and Isaac
Genesis 35:16 – 35:29

They moved on from Bethel, which was a good distance from Ephrath, Rachel started giving birth to another child. This time, she was having difficulty in the delivery. During the process, she was dying. But, before she breathed her last breath, she named her newborn son Ben-Oni. I don't think Jacob liked this name too much, so he gave him one that sounded better. He named him Benjamin. Maybe Jacob didn't want his son to have a name that sounded like it came from the movie Star Wars. But, movies weren't invented yet, so he must have had other reasons.

Rachel died and was buried on the way to Euphrath (which is called Jerusalem). Jacob (now Israel) placed a pillar over her tomb which has her name marked on it. He now takes on the full responsibility of raising a newborn child on his own. I imagine this was stressful.

Newborn babies can't speak. All they do is make demands and cry about it until you figure out what they need. This takes patience and determination. Many of us menfolk don't have these traits when it comes to raising children. We would rather pass this crying child on over to it's mother. Let her deal with it. Israel (aka Jacob) didn't have this option. He was probably around a 100 years old and now an old traveler with a baby on his fragile hip.

Israel (aka Jacob) moved on again and pitched his tent beyond Migdal Eder. While he lived there, his son Reuban (Leah's child) decides to sleep with his father's concubine. Bilhah (Rachel's maidservant) and Israel (Jacob) heard about this. But, the Bible doesn't mention anything more about it. Instead, it retells the twelve sons born to Jacob (Israel) in Paddan Aram:

The sons of Leah
- Reuben
- Simeon

139

- Levi
- Judah
- Issachar
- Zebulun

The sons of Rachel
- Joseph
- Benjamin

The sons of Bilhah (Rachel's maidservant)
- Dan
- Naphtali

The sons of Zilpah (Leah's maidservant)
- Gad
- Asher

Jacob came home to live with his father, Isaac, in Mamre (near Kiriath Arba (Hebron). Isaac died at the age of 180 years old. His sons, Esau and Jacob, buried him.

Esau's Descendants
Genesis 36:1 – 36:30

Esau had another name. It was Edom, which simply means 'red'. Esau was wealthy and had accumulated a lot of stuff. Even though he and his brother, Jacob, had made things right between them, they couldn't live close together on the same patch of land. Esau lived a good distance from Jacob because of the amount livestock they both had accumulated. They needed space in order to support their farm animals. Esau lived in the hill country of Seir. His people would be called Edomites.

He had a few wives that he had picked from Canaan. Here's the genealogy of Esau from these verses:

Adah

1. Eliphaz
- Teman
- Omar
- Zepho
- Gatam
- Kenaz
- Amalek (born to Timna, Eliphaz's concubine)

Basemath

1. Reuel
- Nahath
- Zerah
- Shammah-Mizzah

Oholibamah

1. Jeush
2. Jalam
3. Korah

According to the verses, all of Esau's sons grew up to become chiefs (heads of a clan). They were in charge of other people living with them in their section of land.

Also included in these verses is a genealogy of Seir, the Horite. Why would the Bible want to include his family tree? It's because Esau intermarried with them in Canaan. Now, we have to know that side of the family, too. Here are Seir's descendants (the Horites):

1. **Lotan** – a Horite chief
- Hori
- Homam
2. **Timna** (Lotan's sister)
3. **Shobal** – a Horite chief

- Alvan
- Manahath
- Ebal
- Shepho
- Onam
4. **Zibeon** – a Horite chief
- Aiah
- Anah – a Horite chief
  - Dishon – a Horite chief
    - Hemdan
    - Eshban
    - Ithran
    - Keran
  - Oholibamah
5. **Ezer** – a Horite chief
- Bilhan
- Zaavan
- Akan
6. **Dishan** – a Horite chief
- Uz
- Aran

The Rulers of Edom
Genesis 36:31 – 36:43

This is a list of kings that reigned in Edom before any Israelite king reigned. These are in order according to the verses:

1. **Bela** – son of Beor. His city was named Dinhabah.
2. **Jobab** – son of Zerah from Bozrah.
3. **Hushum** – from the land of Temanites.
4. **Habab** – son of Bedad. His city was named Avith.
5. **Samlah** – from Masrekah.

6. **Shaul** – from Rehoboth.
7. **Baal-Hanan** – son of Acbor
8. **Hadad** – his city was named Pau. His wife;s name was Mehetabel (daughter of Matred: the daughter of Me-Zahab,)

This is a list of chiefs (KJV: dukes) descended from Esau:

1. **Timna**
2. **Alvah**
3. **Jetheth**
4. **Oholibamah**
5. **Elah**
6. **Pinon**
7. **Kenaz**
8. **Teman**
9. **Mibzar**
10. **Magdiel**
11. **Iram**

Even though it doesn't actually say, is Chief (Duke) Timna a girl? Because previously it mentions that name as 'Lotan's sister'. Could these two be one in the same? If so, this would be a leadership role that they didn't normally give to a woman back in the day. I thought that was cool.

The Story Of Joseph

Joseph's Dreams

Genesis 37:1 – 37:11

Jacob lived in the land of Canaan – the place where his father lived. Let's try and remember that God had changed his name to Israel. From this point on, whenever we say Israel, we are talking about 'aka Jacob'. Cool?

Israel had a son name Joseph. He loved this boy. Actually, the Bible says that he loved him more than any of his other sons. It was because God had blessed him and his wife (Rachel) with Joseph at an older age.

At the age of seventeen, Joseph was outside tending to the flocks. He was with his brothers from other mothers – the sons of Bilhah and the sons of Zilpah. These are the sons that his father had with the maidservants of his mother and aunt. These boys hated Joseph and were mean to him. They probably knew that their father (Israel) gave him special treatment and they resented it.

On this certain day, Joseph tells his brothers about a dream that he had. It was a weird sounding dream that did have a meaning:

"We were binding sheaves of grain. Then all of a sudden, my sheaf rose and stood straight up. Y'all's sheaves gathered around mine and bowed down to it."

His brothers understood the meaning of this dream and scoffed, "What? Do you intend to rule over us?! We don't think so!" This dream made his brothers hate him even more.

And then, probably on another day, Joseph has a dream and tells his father and brothers about it:

"The sun and moon... and eleven stars were bowing down to me."

His brothers were very jealous of him and I'm sure hearing another one of Joseph's tales of 'his greatness' made them want to punch him in the face. Joseph's father thought it was just a silly dream and didn't think too much more about it.

What was the purpose of Joseph having dreams like this? It undoubtedly, made him want to share them with his family, whether they wanted to hear them or not. In the Old Testament, you will read about how God uses dreams to reveal his plans to people that needed to hear them. God may have used Joseph's dreams to let his brothers know ahead of time that Joseph would one day be an important person. Yes, they got jealous and wanted to strangle him. Maybe that was the point. Maybe hearing about his dreams is what sparked the idea in the minds of his brothers of selling him into slavery – which is what was needed in order for Joseph to be where God wanted him to be. Keep reading.

Joseph Sold By His Brothers
Genesis 37:12 – 37:36

Joseph's brothers were doing some 'flock grazing' near Shechem. Israel tells Jacob, "Head over there and see how things are going. Come back and give me the details."

When Joseph reaches Shechem, he looks around and doesn't see his brothers. He meets with a man in the area and asks if he had seen them. The man tells him that he had overheard the boys saying they were going to Dothan. So, Joseph heads that way and finds them. The brothers see Joseph in the distance, and before he could reach them, they begin plotting to kill him.

"Here comes that dreamer!" they say to each other. "Let's kill him and throw him into one of these cisterns. We'll say that he was eaten by a ferocious animal. That'll put an end to his dreams."

Reuben (Joseph's brother/cousin – Leah's son) overheard the whole conversation and tried to rescue Joseph.

"Hey! Let's not take his life. Don't shed any blood. Throw him into this cistern here in the desert. Don't lay a hand on him." Reuben says.

Reuben was trying to help poor Joseph and take him back to his father.

When Joseph reached his brothers, they stripped him of his robe. We're not talking about a bathrobe cause that would have been weird. It was fancy – all decked out and nice. It was what the rich people wore. After that, they grabbed him and threw him in the cistern in the desert. Fortunately for Joseph, the cistern was empty and didn't have water in it. That means he wouldn't have to drown that day.

As the brothers were sitting around eating their meals, they saw a caravan of Ishmaelites coming from Gilead. These were Midianite merchants coming down to sell their wares in Egypt. Their camels were loaded down with spices, balm and myrrh. They were ready for business. The brothers came up with a brilliant plan. Instead of killing Joseph, they decided to sell him as a slave to these merchants. Everybody was in agreement. So, when these merchants stopped by, the brothers pulled Joseph from the cistern and sold him for 20 shekels of silver. The merchants loaded Joseph up and took him to Egypt. It was a done deal.

From what I've read, a shekel was used as a unit of weight and as a currency used in Israel. Since the brothers 'sold' Joseph for 20 shekels of silver, it tells me that they sold him for money. In today's market, 20 shekels is approximately the equivalent of about $6.00. That's sad. That would mean they sold their brother for the price of a Value Meal at Mickey D's.

When Reuben returned to the cistern, he saw that Joseph wasn't there. He was upset, but not because of what happened to Joseph. I think he was more concerned about what his father would do and say to him. So, all of the brothers got together and schemed another plan. They took Joseph's fancy robe and slaughtered a goat. They dipped the robe in the goat's blood and took it to their father. They didn't explain anything. They simply handed him the robe and let him try and figure it all out.

Israel recognized the robe and said, "It is my son's robe. A ferocious animal must have ripped him to pieces and ate him." He was beyond sad. It says his mourning lasted for several days and he refused to be comforted. He took Joseph's death pretty hard.

Meanwhile, back in Egypt, the Midianite merchants sell Joseph to Potiphar. This was one of Pharaoh's officials. He was the captain of the guard. I imagine that's a pretty high position. I wonder if they made a profit from their sell. I'm sure they did.

Judah and Tamar
Genesis 38:1 – 38:30

The verses begin with Judah (another one of Joseph's brothers from other mothers — this was a son of Leah). Judah left his brothers and went down to stay with a man of Adullam. The man's name was Hirah. It was there that Judah met the daughter of a Canaanite man named Shua. Judah and this woman get married and do what normal married couples do. The next thing you know, this woman gets pregnant. Unfortunately, we don't know the name of this woman, but over time she gave birth to three sons and the father of these kids was Judah.

I'm sure years passed, Judah get his firstborn son (Er) a wife. Her name was Tamar. But, there was just something not right about Er. These verses say he was wicked. The Lord didn't like his evil ways, so He killed him.

So, Judah tells his other son (Onan) to step up to the plate and fill the shoes of his dead brother, Er. He wanted Onan to take Er's wife (Tamar) and produce offspring for his brother. Onan didn't like the idea. He knew any kid they had together would not be his own, so whenever he laid with his brother's wife, he would spill his semen on the ground. If you've ever taken Sex Ed in school, you know that this isn't how babies are made. The Lord thought that what he did was wicked, so He killed him.

These verses (Genesis 38: 9, 10) is what some people use to tell others that masturbation is wrong. But, I think they have the wrong idea of what this is about. Back in the day, a widow needed a child that would receive her late husband's inheritance. She would also need someone to care for her. It was the law for Onan to fulfill this duty. You can read about this law in Deuteronomy:

If brethren dwell together, and one of them die, and have no child, the wife of the dead shall not marry without unto a stranger: her husband's brother shall go in unto her, and take her to him to wife, and perform the duty of an husband's brother unto her. And it shall be, that the firstborn which she beareth shall succeed in the name of his brother which is dead, that his name be not put out of Israel. - Deuteronomy 25: 5, 6

I believe the Lord saw wickedness in Onan because he chose to break the law and go against God. That's why He killed him. It had nothing to do with the act of masturbation. It was more about the act of disobedience.

Judah had now lost two sons who had a relationship with Tamar. I think he was reluctant in offering her any more of his sons. He told her to move to her father's house and live as a widow. She would have to wait there until his son, Shelah, grows up. I assume he was a little too young for marriage at this time, but one day he would be a man. She could marry him and carry an offspring of her late husband, Er.

A long time had passed. Judah's wife (daughter of Shua) had died. After Judah had recovered from his grief, he decided to go to Timnah to meet with the men that sheared his sheep. He took along his friend, Hirah (the Adullamite). Tamar got word that her father-inlaw was in town. You would think this would be a happy day because Tamar would finally get to see her father-inlaw. It had been a long time. Maybe he had some news about his son, Shelah? Maybe he was finally old enough to marry her? No. Tamar did something very strange. She took off her 'widow clothes' and covers herself with a veil as a disguise. She sat at the entrance to Enaim, which is on the road to Timnah. This would be the same road that Judah was heading.

Judah sees her, but he thought she was a prostitute. The veil had hid her identity. He proceeds to bargain with her in exchange for sexual favors. A deal was made and the unit of currency was a goat. Unfortunately, Judah didn't have one with him. They agreed on a pledge (like a promissory note) that consisted of a seal, a cord and the staff that he had in his hand. Tamar would keep those things until he furnished the goat.

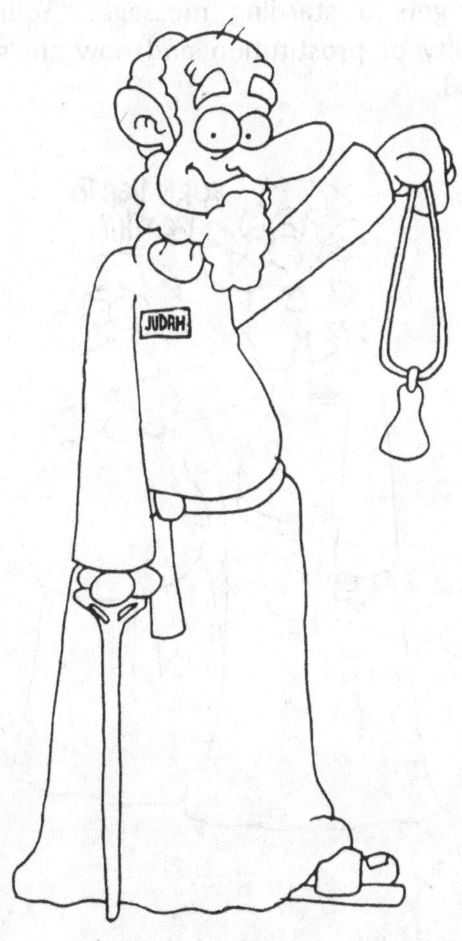

The seal and cord was used in identification that made documents legal. Wealthy people from back in the day had them and used them to mark clay or wax. It was like a stamp, with the owner's signature, that he would wear around his neck on a cord. The staff was probably a personalized walking stick.

Judah gave Tamar the seal, cord and staff. They made the deal and did the deed. She got pregnant and walked away. She took off her veil and put her widow's clothes back on again. And Judah left with a smile on his face.

Later, Judah sends the goat through his friend the Adullamite. He was going to exchange the goat for the items that Judah had pledged (the seal, cord and staff). This guy searches everywhere for the prostitute that Judah told him about. He could never find her and returns back to Judah.

"Uggh. Let her keep it. It's better than being laughed at. Oh well, we tried." Judah says.

Three months later, Judah gets a startling message: "Your daughter-inlaw, Tamar, is guilty of prostitution and now she's pregnant!" This made him mad.

"What in the world! This woman was married to my firstborn son. She's a widow that is supposed to marry my younger son, Shelah. All she had to do was wait. And now she's a pregnant prostitute! Uggh... the nerve of some people! Go get her! Burn her to death!" I can hear Judah saying angrily.

As Tamar is being brought to justice, she sends a message to Judah: "I became pregnant from the man that owns these. (holding a seal, cord and staff) See if you can recognize who they belong to." Judah recognized the items that Tamar had and knew right away that they were his. He felt guilty about it and knew that he didn't do his part by sending his son, Shelah, to marry Tamar like he had promised.

Tamar delivered the babies. She had twin boys. At delivery, one of the babies reached out his hand from the womb. The midwife tied a scarlet thread around his wrist because he was coming out first. But, he pulled his hand back in and the second baby came out first. His name was Perez. The baby with the scarlet thread was named Zerah.

Joseph And Potiphar's Wife
Genesis 39:1 – 39:23

Joseph had been sent to Egypt. He was bought from the Ishmaelites by Potiphar, an Egyptian that was one of Pharaoh's officials. He was in high rank as the captain of the guard.

The Lord was still blessing Joseph. He was always with him and Joseph prospered – even as a slave. He was living in Potiphar's

house. This guy was part of the royal scene and probably had a fancy place with all the fancy stuff to go with it. Potiphar saw all the great things that God was doing in Joseph's life. He saw the success that Joseph had and knew where it truly came from. He trusted Joseph and put him in charge of his household and everything in it. Because of that, the Lord blessed everything that Potiphar had, too.

Joseph was physically fit and good looking. He was turning heads. I imagine the women around him were checking him out. This included Potiphar's wife. She wanted to have relations with him and asked him daily, but he refused and avoided her. He didn't want to break the trust that Potiphar had in him.

One day as he was doing his regular household chores, Potiphar's wife confronted him. She grabbed him by his robe in an attempt to lure him to her bedroom. She wanted some 'bedroom action'. He wiggled his way out of her arms and left his robe behind. I think Potiphar's wife was offended by his constant rejection that she lied to her household servants by telling them that Joseph had tried to seduce her. Her proof was in the robe that he left behind when he ran away.

She even told her husband the story and hoped that he would believe her. Poor Joseph had been framed.

Potiphar believed her story and put Joseph in prison. But, the prison life wasn't as bad as you would think. The Lord was with him. Joseph was shown kindness and favor in the eyes of the prison warden. Actually, the warden liked him so much that he put him in charge of all those that were in the jail cells. This would be another success story for Joseph.

The Cupbearer and the Baker

Genesis 40:1 – 40:23

Pharaoh got offended by his chief cupbearer and chief baker. They undoubtedly did or said something that made him angry. He sentenced them to prison in the house of the captain of the guard. This captain of the guard assigned these new prisoners to Joseph.

For the record, a chief baker was the guy that prepared the food for Pharaoh. A chief cupbearer was the one that sampled it for him. His job was more dangerous because he had to inspect it for poison. What if Pharaoh's food or drink was poisoned? The chief cupbearer would know firsthand because he would be the one laying dead on the floor. For some reason, these two important people from Pharaoh's kingdom did something that placed them in jail.

While they were imprisoned, they both had dreams. Unfortunately, they didn't know what their dreams meant and didn't have anyone to interpret them for them. Joseph stepped up and began with the chief cupbearer. He gave a positive meaning for his dream in exchange for the chief cupbearer helping him get out of prison. All he had to do was mention him to Pharaoh. Joseph's interpretation got the attention of the chief baker. He wanted his dream interpreted, too. Sadly, the meaning of his dream wasn't a good one.

In the end, the chief cupbearer got released and was placed back in his old job again with Pharaoh. Sadly, the chief baker was executed. What about Joseph? Well, the chief cupbearer forgot all about him and never mentioned Joseph to Pharaoh.

Pharaoh's Dreams
Genesis 41:1 – 41:40

Two years had passed and Pharaoh had two dreams. The next morning his mind was troubled. Those dreams had freaked him out. He calls out to all of his magicians and wise men of Egypt. He hoped that they could interpret his dreams. But, none of them could.

The chief cupbearer was reminded of a Hebrew man that once interpreted his dream in prison and told Pharaoh about him. This got his interest, so he sent for Joseph. Joseph was quickly brought out of

the dungeon after a quick shave and pair of clean clothes. I imagine he stunk.

Pharaoh and Joseph meet each other and have a little conversation. Pharaoh tells his dreams to Joseph. Joseph interprets them and gives credit to God for this ability. Not only does he tell him what his dreams meant, he also gives him a way to heed their warning.

Through Pharaoh's dreams, God was revealing to him that there was a famine coming to Egypt. The first seven years would be great. There would be an abundance for everyone. However, for the next seven years after that, a famine would strike the land. Not only did God use Joseph to interpret the dreams, He gives him the wisdom of how to keep Egypt from destruction during the years when the food source was gone.

The plan was for Pharaoh to find a wise man to be in charge of the land of Egypt. He would also appoint commissioners over the land to take a fifth of the harvest during the seven years of abundance. This harvest would be stored in the

159

cities for food. It would be a reserve for the country to be used during the seven years of famine.

The plan sounded great to Pharaoh. All he had to do was find someone to be in charge of it that had the spirit of God. This person had to be wise and discerning. I imagine there was no one to be found. And then Pharaoh looked to Joseph.

"You want the job, Joseph?" Pharaoh asked.

Joseph accepted the offer. This job put him in charge of Pharaoh's palace. All of Pharaoh's people were under full control of Joseph. The only one over him would be the Pharaoh himself. This was a major step up the corporate ladder. This job got Joseph out of the dungeon.

Joseph In Charge Of Egypt
Genesis 41:41 – 41:57

Pharaoh puts Joseph in charge of the whole land of Egypt. He sealed the deal by taking his signet ring and placing it on Joseph's finger. This was serious. He dressed him up in royalty of robes of fine linen and a gold chain around his neck. Joseph also got a company car – a chariot with probably a lot of horse power.

160

Joseph was now in high rank in Pharaoh's kingdom. No one could move a hand or foot in Egypt without a word from him. He had power. He also got a new name. I imagine 'Joseph' was too simple. The Pharaoh gave him one with more of a royalty-feel to it – Zaphenath-Paneah. In addition, he gives him a wife, too. Asenath, daughter of the priest of On (Potiphera), became his wife. Joseph was 17 when he was sold into slavery and spent 13 years as an Egyptian slave and in prison. That made him only 30 years old when he took this big role from Pharaoh.

Joseph did his job well. He stored a fifth of the harvest in the cities during the years of abundance. The verses said there was a lot of food stored. It was so much that he stopped keeping records of it. He was a busy man. However, he did find some time to make some babies. Before the years of famine came, Joseph and his wife had two sons. Their firstborn was named Manasseh. The second son he named Ephraim.

The seven years of abundance came to an end and the seven years of famine began. This famine was everywhere, but in the whole land of Egypt, there was plenty to eat. Joseph opened the storehouses and sold grain to the Egyptians and all of the surrounding countries. The famine was severe all over the world.

Joseph's Brothers Go To Egypt!
Genesis 42:1 – 42:38

As the famine was going on, Jacob (Joseph's father) had heard that there was grain available in Egypt. He looked at his sons and questioned them about why they were just standing there twiddling their thumbs. They weren't moving.

"Go down there and get us some grain so that we won't starve to death!" Jacob tells his sons. I guess they were standing around waiting for a 'grain truck' to drive by and make them a special delivery. Jacob knew that wasn't going to happen. 'Free 2-day shipping with Amazon Prime' hadn't been invented yet.

So, ten of Jacob's sons went down to Egypt to buy grain. Jacob didn't want his youngest son, Benjamin, to go. He didn't want him to get hurt. In Jacob's mind, Benjamin was the last kid that he and Rachel had left and probably was overprotective of him.

Joseph was the governor of the land at the time. He had done moved up in the ranks and was now selling grain to all the people of the land. He was in charge of it all. He immediately recognized his brothers as they stood in line wanting to buy grain. However, Joseph treated them like strangers. I think he was a holding a grudge because he spoke harsh to them.

"Where y'all from?" Joseph asked. He knew good and well who they were and where they were from.

"We're from Canaan and want to buy food." they replied.

Even though Joseph recognized them, they didn't know who he was. Maybe Joseph's appearance changed. It had been 13 years since they saw him last. Maybe they just wiped his memory from their minds and never thought anymore about him. This may have hurt Joseph's feelings.

"You are spies! You are just here to see where our land is unprotected." Joseph says.

"No, my lord. We, your servants, have come to buy food. We are all the sons of one man. We are honest people – not spies." they answered.

"No! I wasn't born yesterday. I know you are here to spy on our land." Joseph says.

"We are a total of twelve brothers in all – the sons of one man. We are from Canaan. The youngest of us is with our father and one is no more." they replied.

Joseph wanted his brothers to squirm and feel some stress, so he had them arrested for being spies. However, he let one of the brothers go so that he could return home to get Benjamin (the youngest brother). Joseph wanted to see him and wouldn't let the other brothers be free until Benjamin arrived. The brothers stayed in custody for three days.

On the third day, Joseph presents another opportunity to his captured brothers that would spare their lives. He said he would let everyone go, except one (Simeon), to return to their homeland with grain to feed their families. In return, they would have to bring their youngest brother, Benjamin, back to see Joseph. This sounds like the second attempt, made by Joseph, to see his brother Benjamin. The first try didn't work because the guy never returned.

Joseph had his people fill their sacks with grain. He also gave each of them silver (as money) and placed it in their sacks. In addition, he gave them provisions for their journey and donkeys to ride on. It sounds like Joseph was making it easy for them.

This was not your normal 'release a prisoner into the world' type scenario.

The brothers stopped for the night and one of them opened their sacks to get food for their donkey. They noticed that silver was in there. The other brothers did, too. They were getting nervous and knew that God was involved in all of this somehow. Ever since they were imprisoned by Joseph, they had felt like God was punishing them for what they had done to Joseph many years ago. And now this? Silver in their sack? What could this mean? Was it a set up?

The brothers made it back to see their father. They told him about everything that had happened to them. Jacob was shocked, especially knowing that this 'royal guy' was wanting them to deliver Benjamin to him. Poor Jacob couldn't bare the pain if he had to lose another son. He couldn't do it.

"Benjamin is not going!" Jacob proclaimed.

The Second Journey To Egypt
Genesis 43:1 – 43:34

The famine was still going strong throughout the land. Jacob and his sons were down to the last kernels from the grain bag they had gotten from Egypt. It was time to go back and buy some more.

"Aight boys. Go back to Egypt and buy some more grain. We're running low." Jacob probably said.

His son, Judah, reminded him of what the 'royal guy' had said about them bringing Benjamin. He basically didn't want to see their faces again unless they brought Benjamin. He was serious. That meant 'no Benjamin – no grain – no food'. Now what?

Israel (Jacob) was troubled. He could risk the chance of losing his son to get food or he could just let his family starve. His son, Judah, offers to help by taking full responsibility of whatever happens to Benjamin if they should take him with them. Israel (Jacob) agrees and allows Benjamin to go with them, but not without some gifts to bring along their journey. By offering this 'royal guy' a few gifts, maybe he wouldn't do any harm to them or their

brother, Benjamin. In addition, they would take a double portion of silver – one to pay back the amount they found in their sacks and the other to buy the grain.

The brothers head out to Egypt in a hurry. Time is of the essence. It's probably because they were starving. They meet up with Joseph. As soon as Joseph sees that Benjamin is with them, he tells his steward to prepare a feast. He was going to invite them all over for dinner. The steward did as Joseph had asked and brought the guests to his house. They were very nervous. Stuff like this didn't happen every day. They were suspicious.

Before they entered the steward's house, they felt like they needed to make a confession. They told him of how they found silver in their sacks from their last visit. They weren't sure of how it got in there. All they knew was that it was there. I guess, in case any silver got missing, they wanted someone to know that they didn't have anything to do with it. Maybe someone was trying to frame them. They wanted the steward to know that on this trip to Egypt, they brought the silver back plus extra to buy grain.

The steward said, "It's OK. Don't worry about it. God put that silver in there." After that, he brought their brother, Simeon, out to join them. Then, he took them to Joseph's house, gave them some water to wash their feet and even some food to feed their donkeys. He was very hospitable.

The brothers learned that they were to be guests at Joseph's surprise dinner feast, so they gathered the gifts they had brought him. Joseph finally arrives at his home and they present him with the gifts. They bowed down to him as the people did back then to royalty figures and they had a little small talk.

"How y'all doing? How's your father? Is he doing OK?" Joseph asked.

"He's alive and kicking." the brothers replied.

As Joseph looked around the room, he saw Benjamin; his brother from the same mother. "Is this your youngest brother that you told me about?" Joseph asked. Overwhelmed by the sight of him, he walks off to a private room and cries. I mean, he hasn't seen his own biological brother in several years. This was a joyful reunion. Unfortunately, Joseph had to hide his feelings because he wasn't ready to let everyone know who he truly was yet.

Joseph washed his face to hide his tears. It was now time to eat.

"Let's eat!" Joseph said.

Everyone at the feast got served. It looks like there may have been some segregated tables. One for Joseph, who probably sat by himself. One for his brothers and one for the Egyptians (probably the royal employees). By law, Egyptians couldn't eat with Hebrews, so everyone was separated into groups. The brothers were seated from the youngest to the oldest. When it came time to serve the food, Benjamin received five times the portion that everyone else received. Talk about showing favoritism! I don't think anyone questioned it. They were probably still in shock for just being there.

A Silver Cup In A Sack
Genesis 44:1 – 44:34

Joseph gave instructions to his steward. He wanted him to supply the brothers with as much food as they could carry. In each one's sack, he would put a gift of silver. And in the youngest brother's sack of grain, he wanted the steward to add his personal silver cup in there along with it. Maybe it was a personal 'going away' gift? We will soon find out.

As soon as it was morning, the brothers went their way and headed back home on their donkeys. They didn't get too far from the city when Joseph tells his steward to go after them. Even though the steward put Joseph's silver cup in Benjamin's sack, he wanted the steward to make it seem like someone had stolen it and question them about it.

The steward caught up with them and asked, "Why would y'all steal my master's cup? Why repay good with evil? This is a terrible thing y'all have done!"

The brothers were confused. They replied, "We didn't steal our lord's cup. We wouldn't do something like that! We know that if one of us stole something from him, they would be put to death. The rest of us would become his slaves. We're not dumb."

"So be it!" The steward demands. "If anyone is found with the missing cup, they will become a slave. The rest will be free to leave."

Each of them lowered their sack and the steward searched their belongings without a 'search warrant'. These hadn't been invented yet. He begins with the oldest to the youngest. He uncovered the 'stolen' cup from Benjamin's sack. The brothers were shocked. They packed their stuff and headed back to the city to face Joseph for the crime.

Joseph was still at home waiting for them to return. As soon as they met him, they dropped to the ground before him in mercy.

"What have y'all done?" Joseph asked. "Don't y'all know that I have ways of finding out?"

"What can we say to prove our innocence? God has uncovered our guilt. We are now your slaves, including the one that was found guilty of having your cup." the brothers replied.

"Nah! I only want Benjamin. The rest of you can go back home." Joseph says.

Judah stepped up and pleaded with Joseph with a long statement. Basically, to sum it all up, he wanted Joseph to show mercy. Judah, who was thinking of the well-being of his father, was willing to take the place of his brother, Benjamin, for the crime committed. Judah would take the wrap.

Joseph Makes Himself Known
Genesis 45:1 – 45:28

Joseph couldn't take it any longer. He reveals the truth in front of everybody.

"I am Joseph!" Joseph proclaims. "Is my father still living?"

His brothers were speechless. They were terrified at the sight of Joseph. The same brother that they had treated so badly years ago was now standing before them. He now had power (equal to Pharaoh) and could have ended their life right then and there. They didn't know what to say.

"Come closer to me." Joseph says. "I am your brother, Joseph. Don't worry about all of the wrong things you have done to me in the past. I realize now that it was all part of God's perfect plan. God knew there would be a famine on Earth and used me to save it. But, it was because of you and your actions that put me where I needed to be."

Joseph told his brothers to go back home and tell their father what had happened and everything that he had said. He told them to return back quickly to him with their father. They would also be changing their home address to live near to him in the region of Goshen. It would be the future home for them and their families – children and grandchildren. They could also bring their flocks, herds and everything they had. This would be their

new home and Joseph would provide everything they needed. Joseph and his brothers hugged, cried a little bit and parted ways.

Pharaoh got word of the good deed that Joseph was doing and was happy to hear about it. Actually, he wanted to be a part of it. He instructed Joseph to offer them the best land that Egypt had to offer. He also provided his brothers with carts so that he could haul his family back on this journey and everything they would need – including new clothes. He told them to not even bother with bringing their personal belongings because the best of all Egypt would be theirs.

170

Here are some of their additional 'parting gifts':

- Benjamin received 300 shekels of silver and five sets of clothes. Based on what I've read about the wages a person could earn back then, 300 shekels would be the equivalent of over 3 years worth of wages.
- Jacob (Israel – their father) received 10 donkeys loaded with the best things of Egypt, 10 female donkeys loaded with grain, bread and provisions for his journey.

The brothers did all that Joseph had told them to do and headed back home to meet with their father. He also told them not to fight on their way back home. I wonder why he felt the need to say this. Maybe he knew that jealousy could set in again and

mess everything up. I mean, Benjamin did get a little more 'parting gifts' than the brothers. Or maybe he knew that they would fight over the responsibility of caring for twenty donkeys on their journey. Maybe they could learn to take turns or work together when it came time to feeding them and cleaning up donkey poop. Who knows?

The brothers return and they share the news with Jacob. They turned his frown upside down. Not only did Benjamin return, but he learned that his son, Joseph, was alive and well. I bet he was on top of the world.

Jacob Goes To Egypt
Genesis 46:1 – 47:12

Israel (Jacob) packed up his stuff and headed out to Egypt. He stopped in Beersheba for a little one-on-one time to be with God. He offered a sacrifice to Him and God spoke to him in a vision that night.

In that vision, God told him to not be afraid to go to Egypt because this will be the place that God will make him a great nation. God would be there with him. By mentioning "...and Joseph shall put his hand upon thine eyes.", God was saying that Jacob would also die there.

Jacob left Beersheba along with his sons, their wives and children. They rode in the carts that Pharaoh provided. They also took their livestock and the possessions that they had acquired in Canaan and headed to Egypt. Here's the names of the sons of Israel (Jacob) that went with him:

1. **Reuben**
2. **The sons of Reuben:**
   - Hanoch
   - Psllu
   - Hezron
   - Carmi
3. **The sons of Simeon:**
   - Jemuel
   - Jamin
   - Ohad

- Jakin
- Zohar
- Shaul

4. **The sons of Levi:**
- Gershon
- Kohath
- Merari

5. **The sons of Judah:**
- Er (died in Canaan)
- Onan (died in Canaan)
- Shelah
- Perez
- Zerah

6. **The sons of Perez:**
- Hezron
- Hamul

7. **The sons of Issachar:**
- Tola
- Puah
- Jashub
- Shimron

8. **The sons of Zebulun:**
- Sered
- Elon
- Jahleel

All of these were the sons that Jacob and Leah had together in Paddan Aram (not including his daughter, Dinah). The total was 33 in all.

1. **The sons of Gad:**
- Zephon
- Haggi

- Shuni
- Ezbon
- Eri
- Arodi
- Areli

2. **The sons of Asher:**
- Imnah
- Ishvah
- Ishvi
- Beriah
- Serah (their sister)

3. **The sons of Beriah:**
- Heber
- Malkiel

These were the children born to Jacob and Zilpah. The total was 16.

1. **The sons of Rachel:**
- Joseph
- Benjamin

2. **The sons of Joseph (with Asenath):**
- Manasseh
- Ephraim

3. **The sons of Benjamin:**
- Bela
- Beker
- Ashbel
- Gera
- Naaman
- Ehi
- Rosh
- Muppim

- Huppim
- Ard

These were the sons born to Jacob and Rachel. The total was 14.

1. **The sons of Dan:**
- Hushim
2. **The sons of Naphtali:**
- Jahziel
- Guni
- Jezer
- Shillem

These were the sons born to Jacob and Bilhah. The total was 7.

It's obvious that a bunch of folks moved and went to Egypt with Jacob. He brought the whole clan and settled in Goshen. Joseph greeted him and gave him a big old bear hug. Jacob was happy, especially now knowing that his son was alive. He could now live the rest of his remaining days on Earth with his family.

In order for them to stay in Goshen, all Jacob had to do was tell Pharaoh that his full-time occupation was that of a shepherd. Egyptians thought shepherds were gross. Because of that, Jacob would probably never be bothered by them and would be left alone.

Joseph and the Famine
Genesis 47:13 – 47:27

There was no food. The famine had taken it's toll on the people living in both Egypt and Canaan. Joseph collected all the money—every bit of it - from the people wanting grain. The people were now completely broke and looking for ways to get food. They made an offer to Joseph to trade their livestock in exchange for grain - this included their horses, sheep and goats. This worked out for everyone for about a year. Then, they ran out of livestock to exchange. What now?

After that year, they came to Joseph with another offer. All the people had left was their bodies and their land. They offered to sell their land and agreed to work the fields in exchange for food. So, Joseph ended up buying all of the land in Egypt for Pharaoh. This did not include the land owned by priests. They were part of a special program where they received a regular allotment from Pharaoh. The rules did not apply to them.

Joseph made an announcement to the people. He informed them that since he bought them and their land, and provided them with the seed for crops, they were to give one-fifth of the crops that were produced to Pharaoh. The other fourth was for them to use as seed and food for themselves. The people were happy about this new arrangement. They were basically slaves to Pharaoh and were OK with it. For them, it was better than being hungry.

This arrangement later became a law and is practiced in Egypt today concerning land. This law does not apply to priests.

Jacob's Death (The Prelude)
Genesis 47:28 – 47:31

Jacob lived in Egypt for seventeen years. He lived to be 147 years old. But, before he died, he asked his son, Joseph, to promise him that he would not bury his body in Egypt. Instead, he wanted to be buried where his fathers before him were buried.

For his sons carried him into the land of Canaan, and buried him in the cave of the field of Machpelah, which Abraham bought with the field for a possession of a buryingplace of Ephron the Hittite, before Mamre. - Genesis 50: 13

According to these verses, Jacob would be buried in the cave of Machpelah. This is the same place that Abraham had bought many years ago. I also read in the New Testament about the death of Jacob. It seems there may be another burial site for him. Check this out:

So Jacob went down into Egypt, and died, he, and our fathers, And were carried over into Sychem, and laid in the sepulchre that Abraham bought for a sum of money of the sons of Emmor the father of Sychem. - Acts 7: 15, 16

But, before we get all worked up about the upcoming death of Jacob and his burial site, let's continue reading. He hasn't died yet. He still has more things to say and do.

Manasseh and Ephraim
Genesis 48:1 – 48:22

Joseph gets word that his father, Jacob, was very sick. He and his two sons, Manasseh and Ephraim, take a trip to see him. When Israel (Jacob) hears of their arrival, he finds the strength to raise up out of bed to greet them.

Jacob sees Joseph and tells him the story of how God appeared to him in Luz. He tells him of how He blessed him by saying, "I am going to make you fruitful and will increase your numbers. You will be a community of peoples. I will give you this land as an everlasting possession to your descendants after you."

After this, he immediately starts talking about Joseph's two sons: Manasseh and Ephraim. But, before we dig into this conversation, we need to know some background information first. As we already know from previous stories in Genesis, while a man is on his deathbed, he performs a ceremony of 'blessing'. This blessing was also when he officially handed over the birthright to the rightful heir. This was usually to the firstborn, unless this dying man felt someone else deserved it. By speaking this blessing and birthright verbally, it made the oath 'sealed in stone' and it couldn't be reversed.

Jacob was dying. His rightful heirs should have been Reuben and Joseph – his firstborn from two different wives. However, Reuben lost his birthright when he sinned against his father.

And Israel journeyed, and spread his tent beyond the tower of Edar. And it came to pass, when Israel dwelt in that land, that Reuben went and lay with Bilhah his father's concubine: and Israel heard it. - Genesis 35: 21, 22a

Now the sons of Reuben the firstborn of Israel, (for he was the firstborn; but, forasmuch as he defiled his father's bed, his birthright was given unto the sons of Joseph the son of Israel: and the genealogy is not to be reckoned after the birthright. For Judah prevailed above his brethren, and of him came the chief ruler; but the birthright was Joseph's:) - 1 Chronicles 5: 1, 2

Reuben lost his birthright. It was given to the sons of Joseph – Manasseh and Ephraim. But, why not to the brother that was next in line – Simeon? I think it was because of his bad character as we will learn from Chapter 49. Remember, Jacob could give this birthright to whoever he saw fit. Joseph's kids were his choice.

Jacob was sickly as he was talking with Joseph. He noticed

Joseph's two sons in the distance. He told Joseph to bring them closer so that he could bless them. Poor Jacob had gotten up in age and his vision wasn't like it used to be. He could barely see.

Joseph presented his sons to Jacob and bowed down. Ephraim was on Joseph's right side facing Jacob's left hand. Manasseh was on his left side facing Jacob's right hand. Maybe Jacob was confused or his illness had affected his thinking, but he crossed his arms and placed his hands on the wrong grandsons' head. Manasseh was the firstborn and should have been at his right and Ephraim, the youngest, should have been on his left. Even after Joseph tried to correct him, we learn that Jacob knew exactly what he was doing. He had blessed them both, but to Ephraim, he gave the greater blessing. He would be greater than his older brother, Manessah.

In the ending verses, Jacobs knows he is dying. He reassures Joseph and his sons that God would be with them after he is dead and gone. It also seems that Jacob is giving the boys some land that he had taken from the Amorites many years ago. Stolen property? Probably not. He said he took it with his sword and bow. That would make it 'conquered land'. Big difference.

Jacob Blesses His Sons
Genesis 49:1 – 49:28

Jacob calls for his sons and tells them to gather around. He wanted to give them some predictions of what their future holds. It wasn't that he was a soothsayer, but you can pretty much tell how your kid will turn out by how they acted when they were younger. It's more of a 'parental observation' thing. If you have a bratty kid that stays in trouble in school

all of the time, chances are, they will be in prison in the near future. Heed the warning.

These were Jacob's last words to his sons. These were the results of his predictions he had made about them:

Reuben: He was the firstborn, but he gave up his birthright by his evil actions. The birthright then moved to Joseph, who received a double portion as the oldest son of Jacob's wife Rachel.

Simeon and Levi: These two brothers were mentioned together as being violent (Genesis 49:3–4). Their land would be divided. This did occur later, as Simeon was given only a few cities in Israel and the Levites were the priestly tribe that received no land inheritance.

Judah: Judah was like a lion and would be a leader of the other tribes (Genesis 49: 8–12). His tribe would later produce a line of kings - beginning with King David and, much later, Jesus Christ.

Zebulun: This son would later be given the land between the Mediterranean Sea and Sea of Galilee (Genesis 49: 13). Zebulun will also have land that extends to the sea in the future Millennial Kingdom (Ezekiel 48: 1–8, 23–27).

Issachar: Verses 14–15 state Issachar's land would be agricultural. True to the prediction, his tribe later inherited the rich farmland of the Valley of Jezreel in Galilee.

Dan: Verses 16–18 note Dan would become a judge in Israel. Samson, one of the greatest judges, came from this tribe. Yet many of Dan's leaders worshiped idols (as in Judges 18) and brought God's judgment.

Gad: Verse 19 simply notes Gad would be effective in military struggles. It is difficult to link this to any direct fulfillment due to the brevity of the prediction. Some have seen a fulfillment of this prediction in the great number of troops who served King David from the tribe of Gad (1 Chronicles 12).

Asher: Verse 20 states Asher would enjoy good soil. Asher's tribe later inherited the very fertile land of Carmel along the seacoast.

Naphtali: Verse 21 mentions that the other tribes would admire him. The meaning of this prediction is unclear, though it may indicate his tribe would have an easier life than the other tribes.

Joseph: Joseph received many blessings in verses 22–26, including a double portion. His two sons, Manasseh and Ephraim, became the founder of a tribe of Israel.

Benjamin: Jacob's youngest son would be a warrior, producing many of Israel's military leaders, such as Ehud, Saul, and Jonathan. His tribe would be known for its warring characteristics (Judges 5:14; 20:16; 1 Chronicles 8:40).

These are the twelve tribes of Israel. Jacob blessed each one of them.

The Death Of Jacob
Genesis 49:29 – 50:14

Jacob gave instructions on where he wanted to be buried. It would be at the same place that his fathers before him had been laid to rest. It was in the cave in the field of Ephron, the Hittite – the cave in the field of Machpelah near Mamre in Canaan. This was the same place that Abraham had purchased from Ephron, the Hittite, as a burial place many years

ago. Many of his ancestors were buried there and now he would be next.

After Jacob gave his instructions to his sons, he died. As we learned earlier, he was 147 years old. This made Joseph sad to see his father die. He gave him one last embrace and kiss. He told the physicians to embalm him, which was a forty day process. After that, Egypt mourned for him for 70 days.

After talking with Pharaoh, Joseph had Jacob buried in a tomb that he had previously dug up in Canaan. They held a ceremony that included a bunch of people — family, Pharaoh's officials, chariots and horsemen. It was noticeable to the Canaanites that lived nearby. Because of that, the place near the Jordan is called Abel Mizraim. After they had buried Jacob, everyone in attendance returned back to Egypt.

Joseph Reassures His Brothers
Genesis 50:15 – 50:21

Joseph's brothers felt that Joseph would seek revenge against them for all of the wrong they had done to him now that their father was dead. They sent word to Joseph that contained instructions from their father. The message was a request for forgiveness. Jacob wanted his son, Joseph, to forgive his brothers for the sin they had committed against him. This message made Joseph cry and his brothers were at his mercy.

Joseph reassured them to not be afraid. Joseph knew that he was where God had placed him. This position of power in the house of Pharaoh was because of God. God took the wrong that his brothers had done and made something good from it, which saved many lives. Joseph wasn't angry with them and promised he would provide for his brothers and their families. He was willing to forgive and forget.

The Death of Joseph
Genesis 50:22 – 50:26

Joseph stayed in Egypt with his extended family. He lived to be 110 years old. He was able to see the third generation of Ephraim's children. It says that the children of Makir (son of Manasseh) were placed on Joseph's knees.

Joseph told his brothers that he knew that he was going to die. He was ready. He lived a good life. But, before he took his last breath, he wanted his brothers to know that God would always be there for them. He would also take them up from Egypt and give them the land that he had promised their fathers many years ago. Joseph made his brothers agree to an oath of carrying his bones out of Egypt after he died.

When he died at 110 years old, they had him embalmed and placed in a coffin in Egypt. Will they remember the oath they made with Joseph about getting his bones out of Egypt? Will Abraham's descendants ever receive God's 'promised land? I guess we'll find out in the sequel... Exodus.

More From A BackPew Review

Thanks for reading this guide. We hope you enjoyed it and will continue to read our other guides in the series. Here is a complete list of our books from the series:

- **What Does It Mean To Be A Christian**
- **Acts: The Early Days Of The Christian Church**
- **Being A Dad According To The Bible**
- **The Prison Letters: Apostle Paul's Letters To The Early Church**
- **Exodus: The Journey To The Promised Land**
- **Genesis: The Beginning, The Fall And The Promise**
- **The Seven Letters: The New Testament Letters To The Early Church**
- **The Gospel From A Four-Sided View**
- **Healthy Eating: A Few Tips From The Bible**
- **Being A Man According To The Bible**
- **A Marriage Built To Last: Learn What The Bible Says About Marriage**
- **How Do I Pray? The Bible Tells Us How**
- **Revelation: The End Is Near?**